IOWA COOK BOOK

Compiled by

Dorothy Smith

I0809454

GoldenWest Publishers

Dedication

This book is dedicated with heartfelt thanks to my husband and family for being my main food testers, and to my son, Brian, for his computer expertise.

Printed in the United States of America

ISBN 13: 978-1-885590-36-7
ISBN 10: 1-885590-36-9

2nd Printing © 2007

Golden West Publishers
4113 N. Longview Ave.
Phoenix, AZ 85014
(602) 265-4392
(800) 658-5830

For free sample recipes from every Golden West cook book,
visit: www.goldenwestpublishers.com
Also visit our additional site at www.cookbooksusa.com

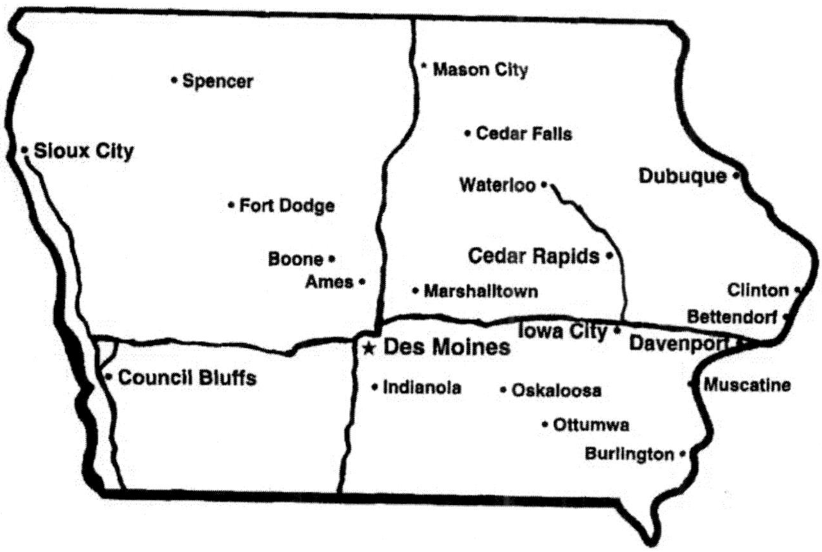

Welcome to Iowa!

Iowa, the heartland of American agriculture, is bounded on the east by the Mississippi River and on the west by the Missouri. Here, endless fields of corn and soybeans dominate the landscape, shaping the state's industries as well as the lives of the people. From this legacy comes the finest collection of recipes, contributed by the residents of Iowa, that you will find anywhere.

From Indian Two-Corn Pudding to Pork Chops Braised in White Wine this cookbook presents home-grown favorites and encompasses both ethnic traditions and gourmet specialties. A special section entitled "Iowa Corn Recipes" highlights the Hawkeye State's most famous export.

From Iowa's tables and hearths to yours, these recipes are destined to become new family favorites.

Enjoy the tastes of Iowa!

Iowa Facts & Information

Size – 23rd largest state with an area of 56,290 square miles
Statehood – Dec 18, 1846 – 29th state
State Nickname – The Hawkeye State
State Population – 2,913,808
State Song – The Song of Iowa
State Flower – Wild Rose
State Bird – Eastern goldfinch
State Tree – Oak
State Rock – Geode

State Motto – *Our liberties we prize and our rights we will maintain*
Geography – The only state bordered by two navigable rivers-the Missouri to the west and the Mississippi to the east.

Famous Natives of Iowa

Julien Dubuque – Iowa's first settler, began mining lead near present-day Dubuque in 1788.
John Wayne – Oscar–winning actor born Marion Robert Morrison in Winterset.
Glenn Miller – Founder of the Glenn Miller Orchestra was born in Clarinda.
Mamie Doud Eisenhower – Wife of President Dwight Eisenhower was born in Boone.
Herbert Hoover – Our 31st president, was born in West Branch.
Donna Reed – Born Donnabell Mullenger in Denison.
Buffalo Bill Cody – William F. "Buffalo Bill" Cody was born in Davenport.
J. V. Atanasoff – Inventor of the digital computer.

Other well-known Iowans

Cloris Leachman, Carrie Chapman Catt, Simon Estes, Hugh Sidney, Meredith Wilson, Grant Wood – and of course, Radar O'Riley of M*A*S*H fame who claimed to be from Ottumwa.

For more information about Iowa, contact:
Iowa Department of Economic Development 1-800-345-IOWA (travel packets) or via the internet: www.state.ia.us

Iowa-Style Mini-Pizzas

2 lbs. bulk IOWA PORK SAUSAGE
2 cups shredded PIZZA CHEESE BLEND
2 Tbsp. KETCHUP
1 tsp. ITALIAN BLEND HERBS
1/4 tsp. GARLIC SALT
1 jar (10 oz.) PIZZA SAUCE
2 loaves FRENCH BAGUETTE BREAD cut into 1/2 inch slices
Grated PARMESAN CHEESE

Brown sausage in a medium skillet. Drain. Add cheese and ketchup to skillet and combine. Cook over low heat until cheese is melted. Add spices and blend well. Spread pizza sauce on each slice of bread. Top with sausage mixture and grated cheese. Bake in a 400° oven for 10 minutes or until cheese bubbles.

Makes 3 dozen mini-pizzas.

Cool Cucumber Spread

1 lg. CUCUMBER, peeled, seeded and finely chopped
3/4 cup finely chopped ONION
1 pkg. (8 oz.) CREAM CHEESE, softened
2 Tbsp. MAYONNAISE
1 tsp. MILK
SALT and PEPPER to taste
2 Tbsp. finely chopped FRESH DILL LEAVES

In a medium bowl, combine cucumber and onion with cream cheese. Add mayonnaise, milk, salt and pepper. Blend well and then chill. Spread on small rounds of bread and garnish with fresh dill.

Iowa Meatballs

2 lbs. GROUND BEEF
1 cup crumbled CORN FLAKES
1/2 cup chopped FRESH PARSLEY
1/4 cup chopped ONION
1/2 tsp. GARLIC POWDER
1/4 tsp. PEPPER
2 EGGS
1/3 cup KETCHUP
2 Tbsp. SOY SAUCE

In large bowl, combine all ingredients and blend well. Shape into small balls and place in a single layer in a 9 x 13 baking pan. Pour Iowa Meatball Sauce over meatballs. Bake in a 350° oven for 30 minutes. Serve hot.

Makes 5 dozen meatballs.

Iowa Meatball Sauce

2 Tbsp. BROWN SUGAR
1 can (16 oz.) JELLIED CRANBERRY SAUCE
1 bottle (12 oz.) CHILI SAUCE
1 Tbsp. mild VINEGAR

In a medium saucepan, combine all sauce ingredients. Heat and stir until smooth and well-blended.

Baked Artichoke Dip

2 jars (6.5 oz. ea.) ARTICHOKE HEARTS, drained
1/4 cup diced RED ONION
1 cup grated PARMESAN CHEESE
1/4 tsp. GARLIC POWDER
1/8 tsp. TABASCO® SAUCE
1/8 tsp. WORCESTERSHIRE SAUCE
1 cup MAYONNAISE
1/2 cup SOUR CREAM

In a medium bowl, blend all ingredients. Place mixture in a small casserole and bake at 325° for 25 minutes. Serve with fresh vegetables and crackers.

Nacho Party Mix

Karen Lichtenberg-Schaller

8 cups CORN CHEX®
4 cups popped POPCORN
3 cups CORN CHIPS
1 cup PEANUTS
1/2 cup light CORN SYRUP
1 stick MARGARINE
1 pkg. TACO SEASONING
1/4 cup BROWN SUGAR

Put Corn Chex, popcorn, corn chips and peanuts in a large roasting pan. In a saucepan, combine corn syrup, margarine, taco seasoning and brown sugar. Bring to a boil, and then pour over cereal mixture. Bake in a 250° oven for 1 hour, stirring every 15

Des Moines

Des Moines is the capital, largest city, and chief manufacturing center of Iowa. In 1843, Fort Des Moines was established at the juncture of the Des Moines River and the Raccoon River. Thesettlement that surrounded the fort was incorporated as a town in 1853 and Des Moines became the state capital that same year. The Iowa State Fair held here is considered America's classic state fair and is Iowa's largest tourism event.

Chicken Almond Puff Appetizers

"I created this quick and simple recipe to help save time during the busy season."

Barbara Stensvad-Chestnut Charm Bed & Breakfast, Atlantic

1 cup FLOUR
1/4 tsp. SALT
1/2 cup BUTTER or MARGARINE
1 cup CHICKEN STOCK
1 tsp. CHICKEN BOUILLON
4 EGGS
3/4 cup finely diced, cooked CHICKEN
3 Tbsp. sliced, toasted ALMONDS
1/16 tsp. PAPRIKA

Preheat oven to 450°. Combine butter (or margarine), chicken stock and bouillon in a medium saucepan. Heat over low heat until butter is melted. Add flour all at once and stir vigorously over low heat until the mixture forms a ball and leaves the sides of the pan. Remove from heat and cool to room temperature. Add the eggs, one at a time, beating thoroughly after each one is added. Continue beating until a thick dough is formed. Stir in chicken, almonds, and paprika; mix well. Drop by teaspoonfuls onto a greased baking sheet. Bake for 10 minutes and then reduce heat to 350°. Bake 5 - 10 minutes more or until golden brown. Serve warm.

Make 4 to 5 dozen appetizers.

Citrus Cooler

2 cups SUGAR
2 1/2 cups WATER
Juice of 5 LEMONS
Juice of 2 ORANGES
Juice of 2 LIMES
1 tsp. LEMON ZEST
1/4 cup fresh MINT LEAVES

In a medium saucepan, combine sugar and water and bring to a boil. Cook over medium-high heat for 5 minutes. Cool. Add citrus juices, lemon zest and fresh mint leaves. Let stand for 1 hour. Strain syrup into ajar or pitcher and store in refrigerator. For each serving, pour 1/3 cup citrus syrup into an 8-ounce glass, fill with crushed ice and water.

Makes 12 servings.

The Hawkeye State

Iowa, nicknamed "The Hawkeye State" and sometimes referred to as the "Land where the tall corn grows," is one of the greatest farming states in the United States. The early pioneers uncovered the rich treasure of the land – its deep layers of rich soil. Iowa ranks first in the United States in the production of beef, pork, corn, soybeans and grain.

Hawkeye Tailgate Cider

1 gal. fresh APPLE CIDER
1 cup firmly packed BROWN SUGAR
3 CINNAMON STICKS
12 WHOLE CLOVES tied in a cheesecloth
2 Tbsp. BUTTER

Combine cider, sugar, cinnamon sticks, cloves and butter in a large saucepan. Simmer until sugar is dissolved and butter is melted. Remove cinnamon sticks and spice cloth bag. Pour into cups or mugs. Serve warm.

Makes 15 servings.

European Tea Mix

1 jar (9 oz.) ORANGE-FLAVORED DRINK MIX
1 container (10 oz.) LEMONADE-FLAVORED DRINK MIX
1 cup SUGAR
1/2 cup INSTANT TEA POWDER
1 tsp. GROUND CINNAMON
1/2 tsp. GROUND CLOVES
BOILING WATER

In a large mixing bowl, combine orange drink mix, lemonade drink mix, sugar, instant tea, cinnamon and cloves. Stir well to blend. Store in an airtight container. To serve hot, combine 1 large tablespoon of mixture with 1 cup boiling water. Stir well.

Quick Breakfast Drink

1 ctn. (8 oz.) VANILLA YOGURT
1/4 cup frozen ORANGE JUICE CONCENTRATE, thawed
1/8 cup WATER
2 sm. BANANAS, peeled
2 Tbsp. WHEAT GERM

In electric blender, combine yogurt, orange juice, water, bananas and wheat germ. Blend on high speed for 25 seconds, or until smooth. Pour into a large glass and serve.

Makes 1 serving.

Christmas Punch Bowl

9 cups BREWED TEA
4 cups GRANULATED SUGAR
4 cups ORANGE JUICE
2 cups LEMONADE
1 bottle (liter) GINGER ALE
1 qt. ORANGE SHERBET
ORANGE and LEMON slices for garnish

Pour hot tea over sugar in large mixing container, stir to dissolve sugar. Refrigerate until chilled. Combine orange juice and lemonade in a 2 qt. bowl and chill. At serving time, pour tea mixture, orange juice, lemonade and ginger ale into a punch bowl and mix well. Spoon sherbet into punch and garnish with fruit slices.

Icy Fruit

Perfect for your morning thermos® break.

1 cup ORANGE JUICE
2/3 cup APPLE JUICE
1 med. BANANA, peeled
1 cup fresh STRAWBERRIES, BLUEBERRIES or RASPBERRIES
1 ctn. (8 oz.) STRAWBERRY YOGURT
1 tsp. HONEY
6 ICE CUBES

In electric blender, combine juices, banana, berries, yogurt and honey. Add ice cubes and process until mixture is an icy slush.

Makes 3 servings.

Weekend Slush

Great for a Saturday night get-together.

1 can (12 oz.) frozen CRAN-RASPBERRY JUICE, thawed
1 can (12 oz.) frozen LEMONADE, thawed
1 tsp. INSTANT TEA
1 1/2 cups SUGAR
9 cups WATER
2 cups VODKA
2 jars (6 oz. ea.) whole MARASCHINO CHERRIES, undrained
1 liter LEMON-LIME SODA

In a large container, combine juice, lemonade, tea, sugar, and water. Mix well to blend. Blend in vodka and cherries (include juice). Place in freezer. During freezing process, stir the mixture occasionally to keep ingredients from separating. To serve, add 3/4 cup slush to each glass and fill to the top with soda.

Spicy Apple Punch

"This is a delightfully refreshing punch for any occasion. I created this to capture the taste of freshly-grown Iowa apples."
Barbara Stensvad-Chestnut Charm Bed & Breakfast, Atlantic

Apple concentrate:
2 cups APPLESAUCE
1 cup APPLE JUICE
2 Tbsp. BROWN SUGAR
1 tsp. ground GINGER
8 cups APPLE JUICE or APPLE CIDER, chilled
3 cups pre-sweetened LEMONADE
1 qt. LEMON-LIME SODA
1 GRANNY SMITH APPLE®, cored and sliced into rings for garnish

In a large saucepan, combine applesauce, apple juice, sugar and ginger. Bring mixture to a boil, stirring constantly. Reduce heat and simmer for 10 minutes. Remove from heat, cool, and refrigerate until ready to serve. At serving time, add chilled apple juice or cider, lemonade, and soda to apple concentrate. Garnish with apple slices.

Makes 3 quarts.

Haymaker's Iced Tea

Nothing quenches thirst better on a hot, humid summer day than a tall glass of iced tea.

6 cups BOILING WATER
6 TEA BAGS BLACK TEA, or your choice
1/2 cup SUGAR
juice of 1 LEMON
juice of 1 ORANGE

In a pitcher or other container, combine boiling water and tea bags. Allow to steep for 5 minutes. Remove tea bags. In a small bowl, combine sugar, lemon juice and orange juice. Blend with tea and let cool. Refrigerate, covered, until well chilled. Serve in tall glasses over ice. Recipe may be doubled or tripled.

Breakfast & Brunch

Swiss Cheese & Mushroom Strata

"This is a hearty dish filled with Iowa products: pork, milk, eggs, cheese and bread. We often serve this to our guests."

Don & Shari Oleson-Shari's Garden Home B & B, Carroll

16 slices BREAD, crusts removed
1 1/2 cups PORK & BACON SAUSAGE, crumbled and browned
1 can (4.5 oz.) sliced MUSHROOMS, drained
6-8 slices SWISS CHEESE
8 EGGS, beaten
1 tsp. DRY MUSTARD
3 cups MILK

Line a 9 x 13 pan with 8 slices of bread. Layer with meat, mushrooms and cheese. Layer remaining slices of bread over cheese. In a medium bowl, combine eggs, mustard and milk; pour over casserole and refrigerate for 12-24 hours. Bake at 350° for 1 hour.

Breakfast Tortilla

Put a taste of the Southwest in your next morning meal!

1 lb. spicy bulk IOWA PORK SAUSAGE
1/3 cup chopped ONION
1/3 cup sliced MUSHROOMS
12 EGGS, slightly beaten
12 (8-inch) FLOUR TORTILLAS
2 lbs. PROCESSED CHEESE, cubed
1 can (10 oz.) TOMATOES AND CHILES

In large skillet, brown sausage. Remove sausage from skillet and drain. Saute onion and mushrooms in pork drippings until tender. Add eggs to skillet and cook until moist yet set. Combine sausage with onions, mushrooms and eggs. Spoon egg mixture onto each tortilla and roll up; arrange with seams down in a greased 9 x 13 baking dish. Heat cheese and tomatoes in a heavy saucepan until cheese has melted. Pour cheese mixture over tortillas and bake until bubbly in a 350° oven for 12-15 minutes.

Serves 10-12.

Breakfast Pizza

This makes an excellent evening meal, too!

1 lb. bulk IOWA PORK SAUSAGE
1 can (8 oz.) refrigerated CRESCENT DINNER ROLLS
1/8 cup chopped GREEN BELL PEPPER
1/8 cup chopped ONION
2 cups shredded PIZZA CHEESE BLEND
4 EGGS beaten
3/4 cup MILK
1/8 tsp. freshly grated BLACK PEPPER

In a heavy skillet, brown and crumble sausage; remove and drain. Line a greased 9 x 13 baking dish with the crescent roll dough; press edges together to seal. Sprinkle the sausage, peppers, onion, and cheese blend over the dough. In a medium bowl, combine the eggs, milk and pepper. Pour over sausage and cheese. Bake in a 425° oven for 15 minutes.

Serves 6-8.

Three Grain Pancakes

2 cups REGULAR OATMEAL
2 cups BUTTERMILK
2 Tbsp. HONEY
3 EGG YOLKS
1/4 cup VEGETABLE OIL
1/2 cup WHEAT BRAN
1/2 cup WHOLE WHEAT FLOUR
1 Tbsp. BAKING POWDER
1/4 tsp. SALT
1/2 tsp. CINNAMON
1/4 tsp. CLOVES
1/4 tsp. ALLSPICE
3 EGG WHITES

In a medium bowl, combine oatmeal, buttermilk and honey. Refrigerate this oatmeal mixture for several hours or overnight. When ready to prepare, add 3 egg yolks and vegetable oil. Add all dry ingredients. Beat egg whites stiff but not dry and fold into the oatmeal mixture. For each pancake, ladle 1/4 cup batter into a greased, medium-hot skillet. Turn pancakes when bubbles appear (about 2-3 minutes). Cook until golden brown.

Makes 12-15 pancakes.

Broccoli & Ham Strata

8 slices WHITE BREAD
1 cup SWISS CHEESE
1 cup mild CHEDDAR CHEESE
1/4 cup chopped ONION
1 pkg. (10 oz.) frozen CHOPPED BROCCOLI, cooked and drained
2 cups cooked HAM, cubed
6 EGGS, slightly beaten
3 1/2 cups MILK
1 1/4 tsp. DRY MUSTARD

Arrange bread to fit into bottom of 9 x 13 baking dish. Layer cheese, onion, broccoli and ham over bread. In a medium bowl, combine eggs, milk and mustard and then pour over layers. Cover and refrigerate at least 6 hours or overnight. Bake in a 325° oven for 55 minutes.

Serves 10-12.

Western-Style Filled Omelets

Omelets serve one and are prepared one at at time. Be sure to make the filling before starting each omelet.

2 EGGS
SALT and PEPPER to taste
2 Tbsp. BUTTER
2 Tbsp. shredded COLBY CHEESE
1 Tbsp. finely minced PARSLEY

Beat eggs and combine with salt and pepper. Melt butter in an 8-inch skillet. When butter is sizzling, add the egg mixture. Move the skillet in a short, forward and backward motion to spread the eggs evenly. As eggs start to set, use a fork to lift the edges of the cooked portion and allow the uncooked portion to run down into the skillet. Work quickly, as the eggs should be ready for filling in about 20 seconds. Spread ***Western-Style Filling*** across one half of the omelet and sprinkle with cheese and parsley. Fold unfilled half over top of filling and slide omelet onto a warm plate.

Western-Style Filling

1 Tbsp. BUTTER
1 Tbsp. finely chopped ONION
1 Tbsp. chopped GREEN BELL PEPPER
1/4 cup cubed SMOKED HAM

Melt butter in a medium size skillet. Saute vegetables and ham until onions are translucent.

Davenport

Davenport is part of a metropolitan area that includes three Illinois cities-Rock Island, Moline, and East Moline. These cities are called the Quad-Cities. George Davenport and Antoine LeClaire helped to found this city in 1836. Try your luck at the casinos, take a riverboat tour, or visit the Buffalo Bill Homestead or Museum when you visit here.

Cedar Rapids Brunch

1/4 cup BUTTER
1/4 cup FLOUR
1 cup SOUR CREAM
1cup MILK
1/4 tsp. chopped fresh THYME
1/4 tsp. chopped fresh CHIVES
1/4 tsp. chopped fresh SWEET BASIL
1/4 cup chopped fresh PARSLEY
2cups shredded CHEDDAR CHEESE
18 hard-boiled EGGS, sliced
1 lb. BACON, cooked and crumbled
1cup seasoned STUFFING MIX

In a medium saucepan, melt butter and slowly blend in flour. Stir for 2 minutes until cooked and slightly thickened. Add sour cream and milk; blend well. Add fresh herbs and cheese. Cook on low heat until cheese has melted. Arrange sliced eggs and bacon in a 9x13 casserole. Pour sauce over top and sprinkle with stuffing mix. Bake at 350° for 25 minutes.

Serves 12.

Swedish Oven Pancake

Don't miss a visit to the Swedish American Museum in Swedesburg. The museum portrays the immigrant experience from the 1800s to the 1920s.

Ned Ratekin-The Carlson House, A Bed & Breakfast, Swedesburg

2 EGGS
1/2 cup FLOUR
1/2 cup MILK
Pinch of NUTMEG
4 Tbsp. MARGARINE
2 Tbsp. POWDERED SUGAR
Juice of 1/2 LEMON

Beat eggs and then combine with flour, milk and nutmeg. Melt margarine in a 10-inch ovenproof skillet. Pour batter into skillet and bake at 425° for 15 to 20 minutes. Remove pancake from oven and sprinkle with powdered sugar. Return to oven and bake for 5 minutes. Remove from oven again and sprinkle with lemon juice. Cut pancake into pie-shaped pieces and serve with your favorite toppings.

Breakfast Crepes with Herb Mushroom Sauce

Crepes:

2 EGGS
1 cup MILK
1/2 tsp. SALT
1 cup FLOUR
2 Tbsp. BUTTER, melted
additional BUTTER for frying

In medium bowl, beat eggs and add milk, salt, flour and melted butter. Cover and allow to rest for 30 minutes. Heat an 8-inch skillet until medium-hot. Brush bottom with a film of butter. Ladle in approximately 3 tablespoons of batter. Tilt skillet and spoon batter to edge of pan to make a thin crepe layer. Cook only a few minutes and then gently flip crepe to other side and lightly brown. Remove crepe and continue procedure until all batter is used. Film skillet with butter before cooking each crepe.

Crepe filling:

2 Tbsp. BUTTER
1 cup finely diced, cooked SMOKED HAM
8 EGGS
1/2 cup MILK
1/4 cup WATER
1/2 tsp. PAPRIKA

Melt butter in a medium skillet. Add diced ham and lightly brown. Beat eggs, milk, water and paprika together and pour over ham in skillet. Cook over low heat until eggs are thick but still moist. Spoon eggs into center of crepe. Roll up and place seam side down on serving plate. Spoon ***Herb Mushroom Sauce*** (see next page) over the top.

Serves 6 (2 crepes per person).

(Continued next page)

Breakfast Crepes with Herb Mushroom Sauce (continued)

Herb Mushroom Sauce

1 cup sliced fresh MUSHROOMS
1/4 cup chopped GREEN ONIONS
4 Tbsp. BUTTER
1 1/2 Tbsp. FLOUR
SALT and PEPPER to taste
1 cup SOUR CREAM
1/2 cup MILK
1 tsp. PREPARED MUSTARD
3 Tbsp. chopped fresh PARSLEY
1 tsp. chopped fresh TARRAGON

In a medium skillet, saute mushrooms and onions in butter. Blend in flour, salt and pepper. Stir slowly over medium-low heat. Blend in the sour cream and milk. Remove from heat and blend in mustard and herbs.

Iowa became part of the United States in 1803 as part of the Louisiana Purchase. The government created the Territory of Louisiana, which included the Iowa region. Meriwether Lewis and William Clark explored the territory from 1804 to 1806.

Belgian Waffles

2 EGGS, separated
2 cups MILK
2 cups FLOUR
1 Tbsp. BAKING POWDER
1/2 tsp. SALT
1/3 cup OIL

In medium size bowl, combine all ingredients except egg whites. Blend until mixture is moistened and fairly smooth. In a separate bowl, beat egg whites until stiff but not dry. Gently fold into batter. Pour 1/2 cup batter into a preheated waffle iron. Bake until golden (approximately 3 minutes). Repeat baking procedure until all batter is used. Serve with applesauce, maple syrup and fruit on the side.

Makes 18 waffles.

Cheese Rarebit

This exceptional cheese sauce, flavored with dark beer, makes a wonderful topping for toast, waffles or egg dishes.

2 cups shredded CHEDDAR CHEESE
2 Tbsp. BUTTER
4 EGGS, beaten
1/2 cup LIGHT CREAM
2 Tbsp. KETCHUP
1 tsp. PREPARED MUSTARD
1/2 tsp. SALT
1/4 tsp. CAYENNE PEPPER
1/2 cup DARK BEER

Combine cheese and butter in the top of a double boiler, oven medium heat. Stir constantly to blend until smooth. In a medium bowl combine eggs and cream, slowly stir into the cheese mixture. Continue to mix well. Add the seasonings and then blend in the beer.

Farmer's Breakfast Casserole

"This recipe reflects Iowa's cultural heritage in agriculture. Start your day with a big farmer's breakfast and then, off to work! 1998 marks the 25thyear ofourAG-FEST Celebration."

Michelle Souhrada-Cresco Area Chamber of Commerce, Cresco

16 slices BREAD, cubed
18 EGGS
5 cups MILK
1 tsp. PEPPER
2 tsp. SALT
2 tsp. WORCESTERSHIRE SAUCE
2 tsp. DRY MUSTARD
3 cups diced, cooked HAM
4 cups shredded CHEDDAR CHEESE

Spread bread cubes in the bottom of a 9 x 13 baking pan. In a medium bowl, combine eggs, milk and seasonings. Blend well together and pour over bread layer. Layer ham and cheese on top. Bake at 350° for 1 hour.

Nancy's Canadian Bacon & Egg Bake

2 Tbsp. BUTTER
8 slices of CANADIAN BACON
8 lg. EGGS
8 strips PIMENTO
SALT & PEPPER to taste
3/4 cup shredded CHEDDAR CHEESE

Melt butter in medium skillet and lightly brown Canadian bacon. Place a slice of bacon in the bottom of each greased muffin cup. Drop egg on top of bacon and add a strip of pimento. Sprinkle with salt and pepper. Bake at 350° for 15 minutes. Remove and sprinkle 1 tablespoon cheese on top of each egg. Return to oven and bake an additional 5 minutes.

Serves 4.

Nancy's Cheesy Grits

1 1/2 cups QUICK-COOKING GRITS
6 cups WATER
1 Tbsp. SALT
splash of TABASCO®
1/2 cup BUTTER
2 cups PROCESSED CHEESE
4 EGGS, beaten
4 med. GREEN BELL PEPPERS, halved

In a medium saucepan, combine grits, water, salt and Tabasco. Cook until thick. Add butter and cheese, mix well to blend. In a small bowl, blend a small amount of the grits mixture with the eggs. Add the balance of grits and stir until smooth. Spoon mixture into bell pepper halves, place in a medium casserole and bake at 350° for 45 minutes.

Serves 8.

Delicious Egg Slices

This is my version of a recipe found in a very old recipe book. Bacon and eggs are traditionally a very important part of breakfast in Iowa.

Shirlee Butt-Time Out Bed & Breakfast, Hartley

1 lb. BACON, browned and crumbled
2 oz. fresh MUSHROOMS, sliced
1/4 cup sliced GREEN ONIONS
1-2 med. TOMATOES, peeled and chopped
1 cup shredded MOZZARELLA CHEESE
3/4 cup BUTTERMILK BAKING MIX
6 EGGS
1/2 cup MILK
SALT and PEPPER to taste
1/4 tsp. OREGANO

Layer bacon, mushrooms, green onions, tomatoes, and cheese in a greased 9-inch baking dish. Beat together the remaining ingredients; pour over bacon mixture. Bake, uncovered, in a 350° oven until golden brown and set (about 20-25 minutes). Cut into slices.

Serves 6-8.

Note: This recipe can be prepared the night before serving. In the morning, simply bake, serve, and enjoy!

Council Bluffs

Council Bluffs is known as the "Crossroads of the American West!" Visit the Western Historic Trails Center to learn about the Lewis and Clark Trail, California Trail, Mormon Pioneer Trail and Oregon Trail, all of which converged here during the westward movement. Here, too, you will find the historic Squirrel Cage Jail which had a "cage" that rotated to allow jailers a view of all cells. Or, try your luck at one of the three casinos: Ameristar (a riverboat casino), Bluffs Run & Harveys, that can be found here.

Breakfast Fruit Puffs

"Breakfast fruit puffs are like a filled jelly donut. They have the texture of a glazed donut and are shaped like a muffin. You will get rave reviews with these winners!"

Barbara Stensvad - Chestnut Charm Bed & Breakfast, Atlantic

2 cups BREAD FLOUR
1 env. FAST-RISING DRY YEAST
3/4 cup WATER
1/2 tsp. SALT
2 Tbsp. SUGAR
1/4 cup COOKING OIL
1 EGG, beaten
2 cups fresh FRUIT (sweetened), or canned PIE FILLING
3 Tbsp. melted BUTTER or MARGARINE
1/3 cup POWDERED SUGAR

In a medium bowl, combine 1 cup of bread flour and yeast with electric mixer. In small saucepan, combine water, salt, sugar and oil and heat only to lukewarm (95°). Add lukewarm liquid to flour mixture, mixing well. Add egg and continue mixing. Slowly add remaining flour and stir with a wooden spoon to form a smooth elastic dough. Place dough in a greased bowl and put bowl in a warm area (oven, with a pot of hot water for warm moisture is best). Allow to rise until doubled in size. Place dough on a floured surface and divide into 12 equal portions. Flatten each portion to form a circle. Place 1 tablespoon of prepared fruit in center of each circle. Bring up sides and pinch dough closed to form a ball. Place each filled dough ball in greased muffin cups, seam side down. Allow to rise in warm moist area again until almost doubled. Bake at 350° about 20 minutes. Remove from oven and allow to cool. Dip fruit puffs in melted margarine or butter and then in powdered sugar.

Makes 12 puffs.

Joy's Morning Glory Muffins

"I named my bed & breakfast after the book Morning Glory by LaVyrle Spencer. I have a Morning Glory Room and morning glories that bloom in my yard in the summer. I serve these muffins as part of every breakfast".

Joy Petersen-Joy's Morning Glory Bed & Breakfast, Elk Horn

1 1/2 cups SUGAR
2 1/4 cups FLOUR
1 Tbsp. CINNAMON
2 tsp. BAKING SODA
1/2 tsp. SALT
1/2 cup SHREDDED COCONUT
1/2 cup RAISINS
1 APPLE, cored, shredded
1 can (8 oz.) CRUSHED PINEAPPLE, drained
2 cups grated CARROTS
1/2 cup PECANS
3 EGGS
1 cup VEGETABLE OIL
1 tsp. VANILLA

In large bowl, combine sugar, flour, cinnamon, baking soda and salt. Add coconut, raisins, apple, pineapple, carrots and pecans. In small bowl, whisk eggs with oil and vanilla; blend into dry ingredients. Fill greased muffin cups 3/4 full of batter. Bake at 350° for 35 minutes. Cool in pans for 10 minutes, then turn out on rack. Muffins are best if made 24 hours in advance of serving.

Makes 24 muffins.

Basic Quiche

1 (9-inch) unbaked PIE SHELL
1 cup shredded SWISS CHEESE
1/2 cup shredded MILD CHEDDAR CHEESE
1 cup cooked HAM, cubed
1/4 cup chopped ONION
4 EGGS
1 cup WHOLE MILK
2 Tbsp. FLOUR
1/2 tsp. SALT
1/4 tsp. BLACK PEPPER
1/2 tsp. NUTMEG

Bake pie shell in a 375° oven for 6 minutes. Remove from oven and cool. Layer in pie shell, the cheeses, ham and onion. In a medium bowl, combine the eggs, milk, flour, salt and pepper. Blend well and then pour over the top of the onion layer. Sprinkle nutmeg on top and bake in a 350° oven for 45-50 minutes (center should be "set").

Serves 6.

Apple French Toast

"This is a fast, easy and tasty breakfast that can be made the night before. It's a real favorite of our guests."

Joy Petersen-Joy's Morning Glory Bed & Breakfast, Elk Horn

1 cup BROWN SUGAR
1/2 cup MARGARINE
2 Tbsp. LIGHT CORN SYRUP
2 lg. APPLES, peeled, cored and sliced to 1/4" thickness
1/2 cup chopped PECANS
3 EGGS
1 cup MILK
1 tsp. VANILLA
9 slices FRENCH BREAD cut to 3/4" thickness

In a small saucepan, heat brown sugar, margarine and corn syrup until blended and thick (about 5-7 minutes). Pour mixture into an ungreased 13 x 9 pan, arrange sliced apples on top and sprinkle with pecans. In a medium bowl, combine eggs, milk and vanilla. Dip bread slices into egg mixture for 1 minute to soak bread well. Place bread slices on top of apple/pecan layer. Cover and refrigerate overnight. Remove from refrigerator 30 minutes before baking and bake at 350° for 35-40 minutes.

Serves 9.

Granola

Kingsley Inn, a luxurious Victorian inn on the Mississippi River, offers this divine mix.

Nanette Evans, Innkeeper-Kingsley Inn, Fort Madison

2 cups QUICK COOKING OATS
1/2 cup ALL BRAN
1/2 cup WHEAT GERM (refrigerated)
3/4 cup chopped NUTS
1/4 cup SESAME SEEDS
3/4 cup COCONUT FLAKES
1/4 cup VEGETABLE OIL
2 Tbsp. BROWN SUGAR
1/4 cup HONEY
1/2 tsp. VANILLA
1 cup RAISINS

Combine cereals, nuts, sesame seeds and coconut flakes in a large bowl and set aside. Heat vegetable oil, brown sugar, honey and vanilla in small pan. Blend well. Pour over dry ingredients. Mix well to coat all and place in a large jellyroll pan. Toast in a 325° oven for 20 minutes. Pour into a large bowl and allow to cool. Stir in raisins. Cover and store in refrigerator.

Danish Aebleskiver
(Danish doughnuts)

Roland & Peggy Hansen-Hansen's Kro,
Danish Bed & Breakfast, Elk Horn

4 EGG YOLKS
2 cups MILK
2 cups FLOUR
2 tsp. BAKING POWDER
1 tsp. SALT
2 tsp. SUGAR
2 Tbsp. melted BUTTER
4 EGG WHITES, beaten stiff, but not dry
VEGETABLE OIL

In a medium bowl, beat egg yolks and add milk. Mix in dry ingredients and blend well. Fold in butter and egg whites; blend. Add a small amount of vegetable oil to each cup of hot aebleskiver pan. Fill cups 3/4 full with batter. Allow to bake. Slowly turn aebleskiver ball with an ice pick to brown and bake on all sides. Serve hot with sugar or jam.

The U.S. Army built Iowa's first fort,
Fort Madison, in 1808.

Breakfast on the Run

"This can be a quick breakfast for one or an excellent choice for brunch for a crowd."

Jana DeBrower, Executive Director-
Eastern Iowa Tourism Association, Vinton

ENGLISH MUFFIN
sliced MONTEREY JACK or SWISS CHEESE
sliced HAM
sliced ORANGE
ORANGE MARMALADE

For each serving, layer cheese, ham and orange slices on an open-faced English muffin. Brush a small amount of orange marmalade over top of all. Broil 5-7 minutes or microwave on High for 1-2 minutes until bubbly.

Clark's Country Inn Brunch Casserole

"This recipe was given to us by Mary Lou's Aunt Marie when we opened our bed and breakast home. It has become one of our guests' favorite dishes."

Ron & Mary Lou Clark
Clark's Country Inn Bed & Breakfast, Walnut

1 bunch fresh BROCCOLI, medium chopped
1 1/2 cups skinless, cooked CHICKEN BREAST, diced
2/3 cup chopped ONION
3 1/2 cups shredded CHEDDAR CHEESE, divided
1 1/3 cups MILK
3 EGGS
3/4 cup BISQUICK®
SALT and PEPPER to taste
1/4 cup sliced ALMONDS

In a 10-inch pie dish, layer broccoli, chicken and onion and top with 3 cups of shredded cheese. In a medium bowl or blender, combine milk, eggs, Bisquick, salt and pepper. Pour milk mixture over the broccoli mixture. Bake in a 400° oven for 25-35 minutes. Remove from oven and top with the remaining 1/2 cup shredded cheese and the almonds. Return to oven briefly, until the cheese softens but still holds its shape.

Sioux City

The Sergeant Floyd Monument became the first registered national historic landmark in the U.S. Sergeant Floyd was the only person to die on the Lewis and Clark expedition, which explored this region on the way to the Pacific Ocean.

Other places to visit in Sioux City:
- *Sergeant Floyd Riverboat Museum*
- *SHRA Railroad Museum*
- *Sioux City Public Museum*
- *The Loess Ridge Nature Center*

Sylvia's Swedish Pancakes

"When I was a child we often visited our family friend, Sylvia Swanson, in Albert City. It was wonderful to wake up to the smell of her pancakes. We serve this recipe at our inn and it has become a favorite of our guests."

Mary Nichols-Hanna Marie Country Inn, Spencer

3 EGGS
2Tbsp. OIL
2 Tbsp. SUGAR
Pinch of SALT
1 Tbsp. VANILLA
3 1/4 cups MILK
2 cups FLOUR

Place eggs in a mixer bowl and beat until just frothy. Add oil, sugar, salt and vanilla and blend. Blend in the milk. Slowly add flour on low-speed and mix until smooth. Strain through a medium-sized strainer into pitcher. Spray a skillet with cooking spray and pour 4 tablespoonsful of batter onto surface of pan. When pancake is golden brown, turn and lightly brown the other side. Remove to serving plate. Pour two tablespoonsful of Hannah's Raspberry Sauce over the lightly browned surface of pancake and roll up. Pour 3 more tablespoonsful of sauce over top. Sprinkle with powdered sugar and serve.

Hannah's Raspberry Sauce

"This is my mother's recipe, and a favorite of our guests. We serve it with pancakes, ice cream, pastries and even chicken!"

Mary Nichols-Hanna Marie Country Inn, Spencer

1 cup SUGAR
1/3 cup CORNSTARCH
1 cup RASPBERRY JUICE
1 can frozen concentrated ORANGE JUICE, thawed
1 cup WATER
2 cups FRESH (or frozen) RASPBERRIES

Combine sugar and cornstarch and set aside. In a saucepan, place raspberry and orange juices and water. Stir and then add sugar mixture. Stir until blended and heat over medium flame, stirring occasionally. When mixture has thickened, add raspberries and stir gently to mix. Cook over low flame until berries are cooked through. Store in refrigerator or freezer until ready to use.

Iowa Hawkeyes Football Stew

A wonderful stew to enjoy while watching the Hawkeyes play another winning game!

2 Tbsp. BUTTER
2 lbs. BEEF STEW MEAT, cubed
2 cups sliced CARROTS
2 cups diced POTATOES
1/2 cup chopped CELERY
1 cup chopped ONION
1 can (15 oz.) diced TOMATOES
1/2 cup WATER
2 Tbsp. SUGAR
3 Tbsp. MINUTE TAPIOCA
SALT and PEPPER to taste

Melt the butter in a Dutch oven; add the stew meat and brown. Add the vegetables, water and rest of ingredients. Blend well together. Cover and bake in a 250° oven for 4 hours.

Serves 4-6.

Cheddar & Potato Soup

Jim Stevens, President-Maytag Dairy Farms, Newton

1/2 cup BUTTER
6 GREEN ONIONS, chopped
3 stalks CELERY, thinly sliced
1 lg. CARROT, diced
1/4 cup FLOUR
5 cups CHICKEN BROTH
1 lg. POTATO, diced
1 cup HALF and HALF
1/2 lb. MAYTAG® WHITE CHEDDAR CHEESE, grated
1 tsp. TABASCO® sauce
1 tsp. WORCESTERSHIRE SAUCE

Garnish (per serving):
1/4 cup BACON, fried and crumbled
1/4 cup MAYTAG® WHITE CHEDDAR CHEESE, grated
2 Tbsp. chopped CHIVES

In large saucepan, melt butter and saute onions, celery and carrots until wilted. Dust the mixture with flour and stir for 3 minutes. Whisk in broth, 1 cup at a time and add diced potato. Bring to a boil, reduce heat, and simmer 20-30 minutes or until potato is cooked. Remove from heat, whisk in half and half, cheese, Tabasco and Worcestershire sauce until smooth. Ladle into soup bowls and add garnish.

Serves 4-6.

Tavern Crackers

"These crackers were served with soups or stews at inns and taverns in the late 1700s and early 1800s."

Nick Colbert-Historic Old Fort Madison, Fort Madison

2 cups FLOUR
1 cup BUTTER
1 cup BROWN SUGAR
1/2 cup BRANDY or WINE
pinch of MACE or NUTMEG
MILK

Mix flour, butter, brown sugar, brandy or wine and mace or nutmeg together in a large bowl. Moisten with a little milk and knead well. On a floured board, roll out until very thin, cut into squares and place on a cookie sheet. Bake in a 375° oven for 8-10 minutes or until golden brown.

Hobo Convention Mulligan Stew

"This recipe has been used for years at our Hobo convention. The stew is cooked, served and enjoyed by as many as 5,000 conventioneers. Twenty stew pots are used in its preparation."

Esther Higdon-Britt Chamber of Commerce, Britt

450 lbs. GROUND BEEF
900 lbs. POTATOES
250 lbs. CARROTS
35 lbs. RED or GREEN BELL PEPPERS (or a combination of both)
300 lbs. CABBAGE
100 lbs. TURNIPS
10 lbs. PARSNIPS
150 lbs. TOMATOES
2 lbs. CHILI POWDER
60 lbs. CELERY
25 lbs. RICE
1 lb. BAY LEAVES
24 gallons canned MIXED VEGETABLES
10 lbs. KITCHEN BOUQUET®
SALT and PEPPER, to taste

Brown the meat well and divide between stew pots. Wash and clean the vegetables and cut into serving size pieces. Divide raw vegetables and balance of ingredients between stew pots, cover with water and simmer slowly for several hours (the longer the better). Add salt and pepper to taste.

The National Hobo Convention has been held in Britt since the year 1900. Every year on the 2nd Saturday in August, there is a parade, antique and classic car show, coronation of the Hobo King & Queen, flea market and plenty of Mulligan Stew! The Britt Hobo Museum depicts the history of the relationship between hobos and railroads in the United States.

Mulligan Stew

(Family size Hobo Stew)

Esther Higdon-Britt Chamber of Commerce, Britt

2 lb. GROUND BEEF
6 POTATOES
6 CARROTS
1 lg. GREEN BELL PEPPER
1 lg. RED BELL PEPPER
1 head CABBAGE
2 TURNIPS
1 PARSNIP
6 lg. TOMATOES
2 Tbsp. CHILI POWDER
2 cups RICE
1 stalk CELERY
2 BAY LEAVES
2 Tbsp. KITCHEN BOUQUET®
SALT and PEPPER, to taste

Brown the meat well and place in a large kettle. Wash and clean the vegetables and cut into serving size pieces. Add all vegetables to kettle and cover with water. Add balance of ingredients and simmer slowly for several hours, the longer the better. Add salt and pepper. Remove bay leaves before serving.

Iowa-Style Beef & Beans

"This beef and bean duo is very versatile. Use it to make a Southwestern-style chili or an Italian-inspired soup."

Iowa Beef Industry Council, Ames

2 1/2 lbs. BEEF STEW MEAT, cut into 3/4-inch pieces
1 can (15 1/2 oz.) KIDNEY BEANS, drained and rinsed
1 can (15 1/2 oz.) GREAT NORTHERN BEANS, drained, and rinsed
2 cans (14 1/2 oz. ea.) diced TOMATOES with GARLIC & ONION, undrained
SALT and PEPPER to taste

In a slow cooker, combine all ingredients and mix thoroughly. Cover and cook on low heat for 8-9 hours or until beef is tender (no stirring is necessary during cooking.) Divide beef mixture evenly in half (approx. 5 cups per portion). Use one portion of beef mixture to prepare 10-Minute Beefy Chili or Easy Beef, Vegetable & Tortellini Soup (see next page). Cover and store remaining portion for later use (may be kept 4 days in refrigerator or frozen).

Easy Beef, Vegetable & Tortellini Soup

It's an Italian soup in minutes!

Iowa Beef Industry Council-Ames

1 portion (approx. 5 cups) BEEF & BEANS (see page 34)
2 cans (14.5 oz. ea.) BEEF BROTH
2 cups frozen MIXED VEGETABLES (broccoli, red bell peppers, onions or mushrooms)
1 cup frozen CHEESE TORTELLINI
3/4 tsp. dried ITALIAN SEASONING
grated PARMESAN CHEESE

In large saucepan or Dutch oven, combine beef mixture, broth, vegetables, tortellini and Italian seasoning. Bring to a boil. Reduce heat to medium and cook, stirring occasionally, 8-10 minutes or until vegetables and tortellini are tender. Garnish with grated cheese.

Serves 4.

10-Minute Beefy Chili

"Just serve cornbread to complete this quick and delicious chili supper."

Iowa Beef Industry Council-Ames

1 Portion (approx. 5 cups) BEEF & BEANS (see page 34)
1 jar (16 oz.) prepared PICANTE SAUCE or THICK AND CHUNKY SALSA
2 tsp. CHILI POWDER
Chopped GREEN ONION
SOUR CREAM

In a large saucepan, combine beef mixture, picante sauce and chili powder. Cook over medium-high heat 5-6 minutes or until hot, stirring occasionally. Garnish with green onion and dollops of sour cream.

Serves 4.

Cheese & Wild Rice Potato Soup

"We raised 4 daughters on our farm and our family always enjoyed a good hot bowl of soup in the winter."

Wayne & Norene Moreland-Audubon

1/4 cup chopped ONION
1/2 lb. BACON or HAM, cut up
3 cans (10.75 oz. ea.) CREAM of POTATO SOUP
4 cans (12 oz. ea.) MILK
2 cups cooked WILD RICE
2 1/2 cups cubed VELVEETA® CHEESE
CARROT CURLS for garnish

Brown onion and meat in skillet until crisp. Drain off excess fat. In medium saucepan, combine soup, milk, meat mixture, cooked wild rice and cheese over medium heat. Stir continuously until cheese is melted. Garnish each bowl with a carrot curl.

Gazpacho

1 RED BELL PEPPER, seeded, chunked
1 medium CUCUMBER, peeled, seeded, chunked
2 1/2 cups canned or frozen VEGETABLE JUICE
3/4 cup mild SALSA
1/2 cup CHICKEN BROTH
1/2 cup fresh PARSLEY
2 med. cloves GARLIC, minced
2 Tbsp. BURGUNDY WINE
1 Tbsp. OLIVE OIL
1/2 tsp. CUMIN
SALT and PEPPER to taste

In blender or food processor bowl, blend pepper and cucumber into medium-coarse puree. Blend remainder of ingredients with chopped vegetables and store in a tight container in refrigerator until well chilled (overnight is best). Serve in chilled bowls with crisp croutons..

Serves 4.

Yummy Apple Salad

"This recipe is a family favorite. The Small's Fruit Farm is comprised of 70 acres of apples and has other fruits and vegetables in smaller quantities."

Joyce Small-Mondamin

4 lg. RED or GOLDEN DELICIOUS APPLES, partly peeled, cored and cut into chunks
1 cup quartered SEEDLESS RED or GREEN GRAPES
1 cup chunked fresh PEACHES or PEARS (or combination of both)
2 or 3 BANANAS, sliced
1 cup chopped CELERY
1/4 cup chopped PECANS
1 cup MINIATURE MARSHMALLOWS

Dressing:
1 ctn. (8 oz.) COOL WHIP®
1/2 cup MAYONNAISE
1 tsp. VANILLA
2 or 3 pkts. EQUAL®

In a large bowl, combine all fruits, celery, nuts and marshmallows. Combine all dressing ingredients together in a bowl, then fold into the fruit mixture. Chill until ready to serve.

Note: During the winter months, if fresh fruit is not available, use drained fruit cocktail or a combination of canned fruits with the chopped apples.

Hiatt Orchard, East Peru

The red Delicious apple, the top-selling pineapple in the United States, was developed in an orchard near East Peru, Iowa. Shoots from the stump of a stray apple tree began producing fruit in Jesse Hiatt's orchard in the 1880s Hiatt entered the new variety, which he called the "Hawkeye" apple, in an apple contest and won. In 1895, Stark Brothers Nursery purchased rights to the apple, renaming it Delicious. Offshoots of the orginal tree still produce apples on the same site.

Iowa Garden Macaroni Salad

1 cup SHELL MACARONI, uncooked
1 cup TWIRL MACARONI, uncooked
1 cup MOSTACCIOLI MACARONI, uncooked
1 med. RED ONION, cut into rings
1 med. TOMATO, chopped
1/2 cup CELERY, chopped
1 GREEN BELL PEPPER, cut into rings
1/2 cup chopped RADISHES
1/2 cup thinly sliced CARROTS
3/4 cup RIPE PITTED OLIVES
1/3 cup fresh HERBS (combination of PARSLEY, CHIVES and TARRAGON)
SALT and PEPPER to taste

In large kettle combine pastas and cook according to directions. Drain in a colander and rinse with cold water to cool quickly. In a large salad bowl, combine the cooled pastas with vegetables, herbs and seasonings. Blend the following ***Olive Oil Dressing*** into salad ingredients.

Olive Oil Dressing

1/3 cup OLIVE OIL
3 Tbsp. CIDER VINEGAR
2 Tbsp. LEMON JUICE
1 CLOVE GARLIC, minced
1 tsp. dried OREGANO
3 tsp. SUGAR
SALT and PEPPER to taste

In a small bowl, combine all dressing ingredients and whisk together. Pour over the pasta/vegetable mixture and toss gently to coat. Refrigerate until ready to serve. Just before serving mix salad gently again.

Serves 10-12.

Summer Melon Mix with Honey-Rum Sauce

3 cups cubed WATERMELON
3 cups cubed CANTALOUPE
3 cups cubed HONEYDEW
3 cups SEEDLESS GRAPES
3 cups PINEAPPLE CHUNKS
3 cups halved STRAWBERRIES

In a large bowl (or carved watermelon bowl), combine the fruits and refrigerate. At serving time, drizzle with the following ***Honey-Rum Sauce.***

Honey-Rum Sauce

2/3 cup HONEY
1/2 cup DARK RUM
3 Tbsp. BUTTER
1/8 tsp. SALT

In medium saucepan, combine all ingredients and bring to a boil. Remove from heat and cool until ready to serve.

Holiday Cranbrosia

2 cups fresh CRANBERRIES, ground
3/4 cup SUGAR
1 can (11 oz.) MANDARIN ORANGES, drained
1 can (8 oz.) CRUSHED PINEAPPLE, drain and reserve juice
1 lg. BANANA, chopped
2 env. UNFLAVORED GELATIN
PINEAPPLE JUICE and WATER, to equal 3/4 cup
1 cup SOUR CREAM
1 cup WHIPPING CREAM, whipped

Wash cranberries and grind in food processor to a coarse texture. In medium size bowl, combine the cranberries and sugar and mix thoroughly to dissolve sugar. Add the oranges, pineapple and banana chunks. In a small saucepan, combine the gelatin with pineapple juice mixture and place over medium-low heat. Heat, stirring constantly to dissolve gelatin (do not boil.) Remove from heat, cool and add to the fruit. Fold in the sour cream and whipped cream. Pour into an 8x11 pan. Chill until firm. Slice into squares and place on a finely chopped bed of lettuce.

Serves 6-8.

Dream Fruit Salad

"This is a favorite of our family, and so easy to make."

Lorraine Christiansen-Christiansen Family Farm, Denison

2 pkgs. (1.3 oz. ea.) DREAM WHIP®, prepared as directed
1 box (3.4 oz.) INSTANT VANILLA or LEMON PUDDING
1 can (8 oz.) CRUSHED PINEAPPLE & JUICE
1 can (11 oz.) MANDARIN ORANGES, drained
1 tsp. VANILLA
1/4 tsp. SALT
1 cup MINIATURE MARSHMALLOWS
1/2 cup NUTMEATS, chopped

In medium bowl, combine prepared Dream Whip with pudding and fruit. Add vanilla, salt, marshmallows and nutmeats. Chill until ready to serve.

Note: Fruit cocktail may be added or substituted for part of the canned fruit.

The Christiansen Family Farm, Hanover Township

The Christiansen family farm is located in Hanover township, Section 28, in Crawford County Iowa. It was purchased in 1903 by Hans Christiansen, an immigrant from Germany. Hans and his large family, including one-year-old Max, arrived from Germany in 1898. The farm, now in it's 4th generation of family ownership, continued with Max, Max's son Norman and now his great-grandson Gary Christiansen. These days the main crops are corn and soybeans.

Iowa Salad Bowl

Iowa's gardens yield up plenty of the following vegetables.

6 cups MIXED GREENS: iceberg and romaine lettuce and spinach
8 fresh GREEN ONIONS, chopped
3 CARROTS, sliced
10 RADISHES, sliced
1 medium ZUCCHINI, sliced
2 TOMATOES, cubed
1 med. CUCUMBER, sliced

In large salad bowl combine all salad ingredients; chill. Before serving toss with the following Green Salad Dressing.

Green Salad Dressing

1/2 cup APPLE JELLY or RASPBERRY JELLY
1/2 cup VEGETABLE OIL
1/4 cup LEMON JUICE
1/2 tsp. GARLIC SALT

In a medium bowl combine jelly and remaining ingredients. Whisk to blend well. Chill until ready to serve.

Frozen Fruit Salad

1 pkg. (4 oz.) CREAM CHEESE, softened
1/2 cup MAYONNAISE
1 can (8 oz.) CRUSHED PINEAPPLE, drained
1 can (15 oz.) FRUIT COCKTAIL, drained
1/2 cup halved MARASCHINO CHERRIES
2 cups MINIATURE MARSHMALLOWS
1 cup WHIPPING CREAM, whipped

In a large mixing bowl, combine the cream cheese and mayonnaise and blend well. Add the drained fruits and marshmallows. Fold in the whipped cream. Blend ingredients together well and pour into an 11 x 8 pan. Place pan in freezer. Remove from freezer 1/2 hour before serving time, cut into squares and place each on a lettuce leaf. Garnish with a dollop of whipped cream, and sprinkle with maraschino cherry halves and nutmeats.

Serves 8-10.

Hill-Top Grill

A delicious salad meal.

6 cups MIXED GREENS;
Iceberg, red-leaf and romaine lettuce and spinach
1 RED ONION, cut into rings
3 CARROTS, julienne
1 CUCUMBER, peeled, seeded, sliced
2 med. TOMATOES, sliced
6 CHICKEN BREASTS, grilled and julienne

In large salad bowl, combine mixed greens; layer over greens the prepared vegetables and top with chicken. Serve with ***Green Goddess Dressing*** (see below)

Serves 6.

Green Goddess Dressing

1 cup MAYONNAISE
3 Tbsp. CHIVES, finely chopped
1 clove GARLIC, minced
1 Tbsp. LEMON JUICE
3 Tbsp. VINEGAR
1/4 cup chopped PARSLEY
2 Tbsp. chopped, fresh TARRAGON
SALT and PEPPER to taste
3 Tbsp. chopped ANCHOVY, or ANCHOVY paste
1/2 cup HALF and HALF

In a medium bowl place all the dressing ingredients, whisk together to blend well. Store in refrigerator in covered container until ready to use.

Red-Top Creme-de-la-Creme

A tasty, as well as pretty, holiday treat.

1 pkg. (3 oz.) LEMON GELATIN
1 cup BOILING WATER
10 MARSHMALLOWS
1 cup WHIPPING CREAM, whipped
1/4 cup MAYONNAISE
1/2 cup diced CELERY
1/2 cup grated AMERICAN CHEESE
1 can (8 oz.) CRUSHED PINEAPPLE, undrained
1 pkg. (3 oz.) STRAWBERRY GELATIN
1 cup BOILING WATER
2/3 cup COLD WATER

In a medium bowl, combine lemon gelatin with boiling water. Add marshmallows and blend until marshmallows are almost dissolved. Chill mixture until consistency of unbeaten egg whites. In small bowl, combine whipping cream and mayonnaise. Fold mixture into lemon gelatin with celery, cheese and pineapple. Pour into an 11 x 8 pan and chill until firm. Dissolve strawberry gelatin in boiling water, add cold water and blend well. Chill strawberry gelatin until consistency of unbeaten egg whites. Spread over lemon gelatin layer. Chill until firm. At serving time, cut into squares and serve over lettuce leaves. Garnish with dollops of sour cream.

Serves 6-8.

Ottumwa

Ottumwa is well-known for its musuems. The Airpower Museum displays aircraft that date back to World War II. The Fascination Station is a hands-on museum that combines science, history and art. The Pioneer Ridge Nature Area has fishponds as well as hiking, biking and horseback-riding trails. Those who want to experience the open road can take a drive along the Woodlands Scenic Byway which runs through Ottumwa.

Maytag Blue Cheese Dressing

Jim Stevens, President – Maytag Dairy Farms, Newton

1 pkg. (4 oz.) MAYTAG® BLUE CHEESE
1 cup MAYONNAISE
3 Tbsp. SOUR CREAM
2 tsp. LEMON JUICE
dash of SALT
1-2 drops WORCESTERSHIRE SAUCE
1-2 drops TABASCO® SAUCE
1/4 cup finely chopped CELERY

Break cheese into small pieces and set aside. In mixing bowl, combine mayonnaise, sour cream, lemon juice, salt, Worcestershire Sauce and Tabasco Sauce. Whisk well together. Gently stir in cheese and celery. Do not overmix. Keep refrigerated.

Makes about 1 1/2 cups dressing.

Creamy Salad Dressing

Excellent dressing for spinach greens.

2 cups MAYONNAISE
1/2 cup SOUR CREAM
1/2 cup BUTTERMILK
1 tsp. GARLIC SALT
1/2 tsp. ONION POWDER
2 Tbsp. FRESH PARSLEY, chopped
1 Tbsp. CHIVES, chopped

In a medium bowl, combine all ingredients and whisk together to blend well. Store in refrigerator in covered container.

Orange Chicken

"Allamakee is one of Iowa's most scenic counties. Visit the wildlife refuge, the Effigy Mounds National Monument and the Yellow River State Forests. In Allamakee you can fish, hunt, canoe, camp, hike, cross-country ski and more!"

Lois Fossum-Waukon

1 pkg. (2-3 lb.) CHICKEN PIECES
SALT and PEPPER to taste
1 med. ONION, sliced
1 cup ORANGE JUICE
1/3 cup HONEY
1 Tbsp. SOY SAUCE
2 Tbsp. FLOUR
2 1/2 cups cooked WHITE RICE

Wash and dry chicken pieces; salt & pepper to taste. Make a bed of sliced white onions in a large baking pan. Lay chicken pieces on onions. Make a sauce of orange juice, honey and soy sauce whisked together. Pour over chicken and bake in 325° oven for 1 hour or until done. Remove chicken and place pan on stove burner. Stir in flour and cook to a slightly thick sauce. Serve chicken and sauce over steaming white rice.

Rollini Di Spinaci

Terry Lowman-Lucullan's Italian Grill, Ames

2 pkgs. (8 oz. ea.) CREAM CHEESE
1 pkg. (1 lb.) FROZEN SPINACH, thawed and squeezed dry
2 tsp. SALT
1 tsp. PEPPER
10 LASAGNA NOODLES, cooked
Favorite SPAGHETTI SAUCE

In a mixer bowl, combine cream cheese, spinach and seasonings and blend well. Spread cream cheese mixture on cooked lasagna noodles and roll up. Cut rolls in half to make 2 thinner rolls (medallions). Place medallions in a baking pan over your favorite spaghetti sauce. Bake about 1/2 hour at 375° to heat through.

Fruited Pork Chops

"Cookies Food Product Inc., was started in 1975 by L. D. Cook, hence the name "cookies." Cookies products are distributed in 30 states and in Mexico."

Speed Herrig - Cookies Food Product, Inc., Wall Lake

6 BONELESS PORK CHOPS, 3/4-inch thick
1/8 cup VEGETABLE OIL, to brush on chops
1/2 tsp. ground ALLSPICE
1/2 tsp. COOKIES® FLAVOR ENHANCER
1 can (16 oz.) SLICED PEACHES
1/2 cup APRICOT or RASPBERRY PRESERVES
1/4 cup COOKIES® WESTERN STYLE BAR "B" "Q" SAUCE
1 Tbsp. finely shredded ORANGE PEEL
1/2 tsp. minced GARLIC
SALT and PEPPER to taste

Heat skillet over medium heat. Brush chops lightly with oil. Season with allspice and Cookie's Flavor Enhancer. Brown on each side and then remove. Add remaining ingredients to skillet, stir to blend and bring to a boil. Return chops to skillet. Cover tightly, and cook over low heat 5-6 minutes until done.

Mediterranean Beef Pot Roast & Vegetables

"Fork-tender beef pot roast goes Mediterranean when slow-cooked with herbs and red wine. The pan juices make the gravy extra-flavorful.

Iowa Beef Industry Council-Ames

8 RED POTATOES
1/2 lb. packaged, peeled BABY CARROTS
4 whole cloves GARLIC, peeled
3 to 3 1/4 lbs. boneless BEEF BOTTOM ROUND RUMP or CHUCK SHOULDER ROAST
1 tsp. dried ROSEMARY LEAVES, crushed
SALT and PEPPER to taste
1/4 cup WATER
1/4 cup dry RED WINE
2 Tbsp. CORNSTARCH dissolved in 2 Tbsp. WATER
chopped PARSLEY

In a slow cooker, place potatoes, carrots and garlic. Rub beef pot roast with rosemary, salt and pepper; place on top of vegetables. Add water and wine. Cover and cook on Low heat for 10-11 hours or until beef and vegetables are tender. For gravy, strain cooking liquid; skim off fat. In a small saucepan, combine 2 cups cooking liquid and cornstarch mixture until blended. Bring to a boil; cook and stir 1 minute or until thickened. Garnish beef and vegetables with parsley; serve with gravy.

Serves 6-8.

Ames

Ames is home to Iowa State University where the Iowa Games summer sports festival is held. The University campus is also home to the Farm House Museum, where more than 6,000 pieces of Victorian art and furnishings may be seen. On your next visit to Ames, be sure to visit the Brunnier Art Museum, Octagon Center for the Arts, Reiman Gardens and the Story County Conservation Center.

Cashew Chicken

"The flavor of honey is influenced by the type of flowers from which the bees gather their nectar."

Mary Mallett, Food Chemist–Sioux Honey Association, Sioux City

3/4 cup ORANGE JUICE
1/3 cup SUE BEE® HONEY
1/4 cup SOY SAUCE
1 Tbsp. CORNSTARCH
1 tsp. GROUND GINGER
1 tsp. GARLIC SALT
1/2 tsp. PEPPER
2 Tbsp. VEGETABLE OIL
4 GREEN ONIONS, cut up
3 lg. CARROTS, sliced
2 stalks CELERY, sliced
1 lb. BONELESS CHICKEN, cut into 1-inch strips
1 cup CASHEWS

Combine juice, honey, soy sauce, cornstarch and seasonings. Set aside. In a large skillet heat 1 tablespoon of oil until it begins to smoke. Stir-fry vegetables for several minutes until the onions become translucent. Remove from skillet. Heat the second tablespoon of oil in the skillet until smoking and stir-fry chicken strips until browned and tender. Add cooked vegetables, cashews and sauce mix back into skillet with chicken. Continue cooking until sauce bubbles and thickens. Serve over hot rice.

Serves 4-6.

Iowa Pheasant Bake

Iowa, especially Audubon County, is well known for its heavy pheasant population. Should you be so fortunate as to success- fully complete your hunt, try this easy dish.

1 IOWA CORN-FED PHEASANT
1/4 cup BUTTER
1/2 cup FLOUR
SALT and PEPPER to taste
1 can (10.75 oz.) CREAM OF MUSHROOM SOUP
1 1/2 cups HALF and HALF

Cut pheasant into serving pieces (the breast may be cut into 3-4 slices each half). In medium skillet over medium-high heat, melt butter. Dip pheasant pieces into flour and brown in butter. Season with salt and pepper. In a small bowl, combine soup and half and half. Blend well and pour over pheasant in skillet. Bake in a 325° oven for 11/2 hours, or until tender and cooked through.

Creamed Chicken Delight

"Allamakee County is in the north-east corner of our state. Here, history and nature blend into beautiful parks and recreation areas. Ours is a four-season paradise!"

Jane Regan-Allamakee County Economic Development & Tourism Commission, Waukon

1 jar (12 oz.) CHIPPED BEEF, sliced
4 whole skinless CHICKEN BREASTS
2 cups sliced MUSHROOMS
1 can (10.75 oz.) CREAM OF MUSHROOM SOUP
1 1/2 cups LIGHT SOUR CREAM

In medium saucepan combine a small amount of water with chipped beef and bring to a boil. Drain to remove salt. Place in the bottom of a baking pan. Arrange chicken breasts on top of beef. In a bowl, whisk cream of mushroom soup and sour cream together. Spread over chicken. Sprinkle with sliced mushrooms. Bake uncovered in a 275° oven for 2 1/2 hours.

Chicken Enchilada Casserole

"Use either our mild or medium salsa for this dish!"

Speed Herrig - Cookies Food Product, Inc., Wall Lake

1 lb. cooked and chunked CHICKEN
1 med. ONION
1 cup COOKIES® MILD TACO SAUCE
8 CORN TORTILLAS
8 oz. shredded CHEDDAR CHEESE
1 can (10.75 oz.) CREAM OF CHICKEN SOUP

In medium bowl combine chicken, onion and taco sauce. Tear tortillas into chip size pieces. In a large casserole dish alternate 2-3 layers of meat mixture, cheese, and tortilla pieces. Pour soup over the top of casserole. Top with remaining cheese and bake in a 375° oven for 30-45 minutes. Serve with corn chips or avocado dip.

Stuffed Shells

"Dubuque County has something to offer every visitor. Located on the Mighty Mississippi River, Dubuque offers richness in history and heritage, art, agriculture, farms and fantasy, caves and bluffs, scenery and sunsets-as well as the chance to strike it rich (the home of riverboat gambling)."

Andy Mettert-Dubuque County Historical Society, Dubuque

1 pkg. lg. PASTA SHELLS, cooked, drained, cooled
3 links HOT ITALIAN SAUSAGE, chopped
3 links SWEET ITALIAN SAUSAGE, chopped
1/2 lb. GROUND BEEF
1 ctn. (12 oz.) RICOTTA CHEESE
1 tsp. OREGANO
1/2 tsp. THYME
1/4 tsp. BASIL
1/8 tsp. GARLIC SALT
Favorite TOMATO SAUCE
grated PARMESAN and MOZZARELLA CHEESE

Prepare pasta shells according to package directions. Set aside. In medium skillet, brown the sausages and ground beef. Drain and set aside. Combine ricotta cheese with herbs and garlic salt. Add to the meat mixture and mix well. Spoon the mixture into the shells. Place stuffed shells into a baking casserole and cover with your favorite tomato sauce. Bake in 350° oven for 30 minutes or until thoroughly heated. Sprinkle top with cheese and serve.

Dubuque

Julien Dubuque, a French-Canadian adventurer, was the first European to settle in Iowa. His lead mine, "The Mine of Spain," was just south of the present day city named after him. The settlement of Dubuque began in 1833 and became a town in 1837. Visit the Mississippi River Museum for a taste of the days of riverboat gamblers and explorers. Life-size exhibits and the 277-foot sidewheeler, William H. Black, that is now a national landmark, can be found here.

Pork Chops Braised in White Wine

In memory of my beloved wife, Suzanne McNair, one of the best cooks I ever knew.

Terry McNair-Mt. Pleasant

1 tsp. crumbled SAGE LEAVES
1 tsp. crumbled ROSEMARY LEAVES
4 cloves GARLIC, pressed
1/8 tsp. BLACK PEPPER
4 lean CENTER-CUT PORK CHOPS, 1 inch thick
2 Tbsp. BUTTER
1 Tbsp. OLIVE OIL
3/4 cup dry WHITE WINE
1 Tbsp. chopped PARSLEY

In a small bowl, combine herbs, garlic and pepper and press well into both sides of pork chops. In a large skillet, heat oil and butter. Add chops and brown well on both sides. When browned, remove from skillet and add 1/2 cup of wine, stir well and bring to a boil. Add chops back into skillet, simmer on low heat for 25-30 minutes. Baste occasionally. Remove chops to heated platter. Add remaining 1/4 cup of wine to skillet and boil and stir, scraping pan bottom. Cook until mixture forms a syrupy glaze. Remove from heat and add parsley. Pour sauce over chops and serve.

Serves 4.

Mt. Pleasant

During late summer, plan to visit the Midwest Old Threshers Reunion, "America's Largest Steam Show," with more than 100 operating steam engines, electric trolleys, antique cars, gas engines and farm machines. And, year round, you can visit the Heritage Museum and the Theatre Museum of Repertoire Americana, also in Mt. Pleasant.

Roast Venison with Mushroom Sauce

"Bordering the scenic Mississippi River, Jackson County features four full seasons of recreation. Two state parks, 30 county parks, campgrounds, and recreation areas showcase the county's rugged beauty. Other special treasures include two restored mills and 68 Historic Register sites."

Diane Gravert-Director, Jackson County Welcome Center, Sabula

6 lb. VENISON ROAST
1 envelope DRY ONION SOUP MIX
1 can (8 oz.) MUSHROOMS, drained
SALT and PEPPER to taste
1 med. ONION, sliced
1 can (10.75 oz.) CREAM OF MUSHROOM SOUP
1/3 cup MILK

Place venison roast in middle of a 24 x 24 sheet of heavy-duty aluminum foil, sprinkle top with dry soup mix, mushrooms, seasonings and onion. In a small bowl, combine mushroom soup with milk, pour over roast. Add a second sheet of aluminum foil and seal tightly. Place in a baking pan. Bake in a 300° oven for 4 hours. To ensure the tenderest roast you have ever eaten, do not break seal while baking.

Spaghetti Pie

"Cedar Rapids Freedom Festival is an eight-day, award-winning festival showcasing over 100 events."

Ellen J. Skripsky–Sheraton Four Points Hotel, Cedar Rapids

1 pkg. (6 oz.) SPAGHETTI
2 Tbsp. BUTTER
1/3 cup grated PARMESAN CHEESE
2 EGGS, beaten well
1 cup COTTAGE CHEESE
1 lb. lean GROUND BEEF
1/2 cup chopped ONIONS
1/4 cup chopped GREEN BELL PEPPER
1 jar (15 oz.) SPAGHETTI SAUCE
1 Tbsp. SUGAR
1 tsp. dried, crushed OREGANO
1/2 tsp. GARLIC SALT
1 cup shredded MOZZARELLA CHEESE

Prepare spaghetti according to package directions. Add butter, Parmesan cheese and beaten eggs. Press this mixture into a 9-inch pie pan. Spread cottage cheese over top. Brown beef in skillet, add onions and green pepper, drain grease from mixture. Add spaghetti sauce, sugar, oregano and garlic salt and cook for 10 minutes, over medium heat. Pour mixture over top of cottage cheese. Bake uncovered in a 350° oven for 45 minutes. Sprinkle with mozzarella cheese and bake an additional 10 minutes.

Cedar Rapids

Cedar Rapids houses a wealth of ethnic history. The National Czech and Slovak Museum and Library has the largest collection of authentic costumes in the U.S. Another turn of the century town is located at Ushers Ferry Historic Village. This community is a collection of 20 buildings which preserve the age before electricity and plumbing. The 210- acre Indian Creek Nature Center features restored savanvnas, prairies, woodlands and trails.

Chicken Oriental Casserole

"This is one of my family's favorite dishes!"
Marlys Reuter-Sumner

2 CHICKENS, cooked and cut up
2 cups diced CELERY
2 cans (8 oz. ea.) sliced WATER CHESTNUTS
ONION, to taste
Chopped GREEN BELL PEPPER, to taste
2 cups cubed VELVEETA®
1/2 cup slivered ALMONDS
1 cup MIRACLE WHIP®
1 cup crushed POTATO CHIPS

In large bowl combine all ingredients except potato chips. Put small portion of chips in bottom of greased 13 x 9 casserole dish. Scoop chicken mixture over chips. Sprinkle remainder of chips on top. Bake in 350° oven for 45 minutes or until bubbly and chips are golden.

Serves 8-10.

Chinese Rice

"Lou Henry Hoover [Herbert Hoover's wife] learned of this dish in China and it has remained in the Hoover family ever since. Lou would sometimes add odds and ends like a small can of mushrooms, a tablespoon of parsley or some chopped spinach."
Excerpted from Dale Meyers book Dining with the Hoover Family
Janlyn Ewald-Herbert Hoover Presidential Library Museum, West Branch

1 cup ground, cooked HAM
2 EGGS
1 cup cooked RICE
SALT and PEPPER to taste

Fry ground ham slightly in skillet. Break eggs into skillet and scramble slightly. Add cooked rice, salt and pepper. Mix and heat through.

Frikadeler
(Danish Meatballs)

"This is a special Danish meat dish that was prepared by my grandmother Marie Kjergaard. She fixed it every Sunday and shared it with us all."

Norene Moreland–Audubon

1 lb. GROUND BEEF
1/8 tsp. PEPPER
1 tsp. SALT
1 tsp. ONION POWDER
2 Tbsp. FLOUR
2 EGGS, beaten
1 slice BREAD, broken up
1/3 cup MILK

In a medium bowl, mix all ingredients together with your hands and shape into about 12 Frikadeler balls. Fry in skillet on medium high until nicely browned, turn heat to medium and continue to cook until cooked through.

Sweet & Tangy Goulash

"Much of this section of Iowa has Germanic roots. Goulash, an old-world favorite, has many variations. My mother made a quick version using only the first three ingredients. I have added the rest of the ingredients to suit my family's tastes."

Jolene Wilson-Wilson's Ceramics & Apples, Strawberry Point

1 cup MACARONI (I prefer rotini)
1/2 lb. GROUND BEEF
SALT and PEPPER to taste
1 can (10.75 oz.) TOMATO SOUP
1/2 tsp. WORCESTERSHIRE SAUCE
1 Tbsp. BROWN SUGAR

Prepare macaroni according to package directions and then drain. In a skillet, combine ground beef and salt and pepper. Brown ground beef, crumbling into bite-size pieces. Add tomato soup, Worcestershire sauce and brown sugar. Stir and simmer for 25 minutes. Add macaroni to sauce. Stir. Serve with cheese wedges.

Baked Chicken Breast Supreme

"In Van Buren County you will discover the rural treasures of Iowa. Enjoy this county in the southeast section of our state by hiking the trails, canoeing the scenic Des Moines River, biking past rolling meadows and corn fields. Along the way you will find many rustic inns, shops and restaurants."

Mary E. Muir-Villages of Van Buren, Keosauqua

1 1/2 cups plain YOGURT or SOUR CREAM
1/2 tsp. WORCESTERSHIRE SAUCE
1/2 tsp. PAPRIKA
1/2 tsp. SALT
1/4 tsp. PEPPER
1/2 tsp. CELERY SEED
1 clove GARLIC, minced
1/4 cup LEMON JUICE
8 boneless CHICKEN BREASTS
2 cups fine BREAD CRUMBS

In large bowl, combine first eight ingredients. Place chicken breasts in mixture and turn to coat. Cover and marinate overnight in the refrigerator. Remove chicken from marinade; coat each piece with crumbs. Arrange in shallow baking pan. Bake uncovered in a 350° oven for 45 minutes or until juices run clear.

Serves 8.

Sweet 'n' Sour Pineapple Chicken

2 whole BONELESS CHICKEN BREASTS, halved
1 lg. ONION, cut in thin wedges
1 GREEN BELL PEPPER, cut into wedges
4 Tbsp. VEGETABLE OIL, divided
2 Tbsp. VINEGAR
1 Tbsp. CORNSTARCH
1 can (20 oz.) PINEAPPLE CHUNKS, reserve juice
2 Tbsp. KETCHUP
2 Tbsp. BROWN SUGAR
1 lg. TOMATO, chunked
1/2 tsp. SALT
cooked WHITE RICE
SOY SAUCE

Cut chicken breasts into 1-inch chunks. In medium skillet, saute onion and green peppers in 2 tablespoons oil. Saute until vegetables are crisp-tender. Remove from skillet and set aside. In a skillet, heat remaining 2 tablespoons oil until hot. Add chicken pieces and stir-fry over medium-high heat until chicken is done (about 8 minutes). In a medium bowl, combine vinegar, cornstarch, reserved pineapple juice, ketchup and brown sugar. Add to chicken in skillet and cook until bubbly and heated through. Add pineapple and tomato chunks. Cover; cook over low heat until ready to serve. Spoon sweet 'n' sour chicken over mounds of hot rice. Season with soy sauce to taste.

Burlington

Burlington was Iowa's first territorial capital. Plan time to visit Heritage Hill, South Hill and the West Jefferson Street Antique District – these are must-see historic areas. See Snake Alley, a portion of 6th street that is called the "Crookedest Street in the World" by Ripley's Believe It or Not. Don't miss Burlington Steam-boat Days (June 15th to the 20th) or a visit to Mosquito Park Overlook and Starr's Cave Nature/Center I Starr's Cave Park and Preserve.

Crock Pot Dressing

This makes a good holiday dressing and is a wonderful dish to accompany many of the main dish foods.

Norene Moreland–Audubon

1 cup BUTTER
2 cups chopped ONION
2 cups chopped CELERY
1/4 cup PARSLEY FLAKES
2 cans (4 oz. ea.) MUSHROOMS, drained
12-13 cups slightly dry BREAD CUBES
1 tsp. POULTRY SEASONING
1 1/2 tsp. SALT
1 1/2 tsp. SAGE
1 tsp. THYME
1/2 tsp. PEPPER
2 cans (14.5 oz. ea.) CHICKEN BROTH
2 EGGS, well beaten

In a medium skillet, melt butter and saute onion, celery, parsley and mushrooms. Pour over bread cubes in a large bowl. Add all seasonings and toss together well. Add broth to moisten. Add eggs and mix together well. Pack lightly into crock pot bowl. Cook on high for 45 minutes, then reduce to low and cook for an additional 8 hours.

Baked Crab Salad

"This is a delicious seafood recipe"

Phyllis Jensen-Audubon

1 lg. GREEN BELL PEPPER, chopped
1/2 cup ONION, chopped
1 cup finely chopped CELERY
1 can (16 oz.) CRAB MEAT
2 cups canned SHRIMP or LOBSTER
1 cup MAYONNAISE
SALT and PEPPER to taste
1 tsp. WORCESTERSHIRE SAUCE
1 cup buttered BREAD CRUMBS

In a medium bowl, combine green pepper, onion and celery. Remove all tendons from crab meat and flake. Devein shrimp and cut into small pieces. Blend seafood into vegetables, add mayonnaise, seasonings and Worcestershire sauce. Spoon mixture into a greased 9-inch pie pan or baking shells. Cover with buttered crumbs and bake in a 350° oven for 30 minutes.

Roast Beef Au Jus

"This a good recipe for roast beef, especially for a crowd. The au jus liquid is low in fat, and keeps the lean beef slices moist and tender."

Iowa Beef Industry Council-Ames

1 (3 to 4 lb.) BEEF TIP, TOP ROUND or BONELESS RUMP ROAST
SALT and PEPPER, to taste

Place roast on rack. Insert meat thermometer into center of thickest muscle. Season with salt and pepper to taste. Roast in a 300° oven for 30-35 minutes per pound or until meat thermometer reads 150°. Let roast stand at least 15 minutes before carving across the grain into thin slices. Place meat in a casserole and pour ***Au Jus*** over top. Heat casserole in a 325° oven for 20-30 minutes or until heated through (or heat in slow cooker). Remove meat and serve ***Au Jus*** on the side or serve meat on a bun with ***Au Jus*** as a dip.

Serves 12-16.

Au Jus

2 cups BEEF BROTH or BEEF BOUILLON
1/3 cup BROWN SUGAR
1/4 tsp. LAWRY'S® SEASONING SALT
1/2-1 tsp. LIQUID SMOKE
1/4 cup reduced sodium SOY SAUCE
1 can (4 oz.) SLICED MUSHROOMS, undrained

Combine all ingredients and heat to boiling. Stir until sugar dissolves.

Field of Dreams™
Dyersville

In the summer of 1988, the Academy Award-nominated movie Field of Dreams was filmed just three miles northeast of Dyersville. Today, visitors to the Left & Center Field of Dreams can walk out into the cornfield and even play a game of baseball on the original diamond! The Center is open from April until late November. Call 1-800-443-8981 for more information.

Crunchy Chicken & Rice

"This has been a family favorite for years. It is easy enough for 4-H clubs to make for their food projects as well as for young people of all ages."

Norma Hansen-Audubon

1 can (10.75 oz.) CREAM of MUSHROOM SOUP
2 cups MILK
2 cups cooked, cubed CHICKEN
1 cup cooked RICE
2 cans (14.5 oz. ea.) GREEN BEANS, drained
1 jar (4 oz.) MUSHROOMS, drained
2 Tbsp. chopped PIMENTO
1 cup grated CHEDDAR CHEESE
1 can (2.8 oz.) ONION RINGS

In a large saucepan, combine soup and milk. Heat to just boiling, stirring constantly. Remove from heat and stir in the chicken, rice, beans, mushrooms, pimento, 1/2 cup grated cheese and 1/2 of the onion rings. Pour mixture into a greased 2-quart casserole. Bake, covered, in a 350° oven for 40 minutes. Remove cover, top with remaining cheese and onions and bake an additional 5 minutes or until cheese has melted.

Baked Cabbage

"This German casserole was made in huge amounts and served when neighbors got together to harvest one another's crops. Visit Crystal Lake Cave. You will find over 3,000 feet of crystalline beauty-a natural, living cave."

Doris M. Rubel-Crystal Lake

1 med. head CABBAGE, chopped
1 pkg. WHITE CRACKERS, crushed
1 1/2 cups MILK
1 sm ONION, chopped
2 EGGS, beaten
SALT and PEPPER to taste
1/2 cup BUTTER, softened

In a bowl, combine all ingredients (except butter). Place in a greased casserole, dot butter over top and bake for 11/2 hours in a 375° oven.

The corn recipes in this section were contributed by Lois Ahrenholtz-Ahrenholtz Seed Corn Plant, Manilla

The Iowa Corn Boil

8 EARS SWEET CORN
16 cups WATER
1/2 cup BUTTER
SALT and PEPPER to taste

Husk, silk and wash corn ears and place in a kettle of boiling water. Add butter. Cover and boil for 8 minutes. Keep unused ears in hot water until needed. Salt and pepper as desired.

Corn On The Grill

8 EARS SWEET CORN
1/2 cup BUTTER
SALT and PEPPER to taste

Husk, silk and wash corn ears. Place each ear on a square of aluminum foil. Add 1 tablespoon butter and sprinkle with salt and pepper. Fold and seal foil and place packet over hot coals. Grill 8 minutes, turn and continue to grill until corn is browned.

Fresh Corn Patties

1 cup CORN KERNELS
1 EGG, beaten
1/4 cup chopped GREEN BELL PEPPER
1/4 cup chopped ONION
1/4 cup FLOUR
SALT and PEPPER to taste
4 Tbsp. BUTTER

Combine corn with egg and then with rest of ingredients (except butter). Mix well. Shape into 3-inch patties. Melt butter in a medium skillet and add the patties. Fry over medium heat for 4 minutes until golden brown. Turn to brown other side. Keep warm in oven until ready to serve.

Serves 4.

Succotash

2 cups cooked CORN KERNELS
1 cup cooked GREEN BEANS
1 cup cooked LIMA BEANS
2 Tbsp. BUTTER
1/4 cup CREAM
SALT and PEPPER to taste

Combine corn, green beans and lima beans in a medium saucepan. Heat thoroughly. Add butter, cream, salt and pepper and mix together well. Simmer until ready to serve.

Serves 6.

Ahrenholtz Seeds Inc., Manilla

"The Ahrenholtz roots in agriculture and seed go back to the early 1900s. My husband's great-grandparents, Tillie and Henry, were pioneer farmers just south of Defiance. Each year they would select the best ears of corn from their fields and hang them in their corn crib so that they would have seed to plant the following spring."

– Lois Ahrenholtz

Indian Two-Corn Pudding

3 EGGS, slightly beaten
2 cups CORN KERNELS
2 cups MILK
1/2 cup YELLOW CORN MEAL
1 cup grated MILD CHEDDAR CHEESE
1/2 tsp. BAKING POWDER
2 cloves GARLIC, minced
1 can (4 oz.) diced GREEN CHILES
1/4 cup diced RED BELL PEPPER

Combine all ingredients and mix well. Pour into a buttered 2-quart casserole. Set casserole dish in a shallow pan in which 1 inch of hot water has been placed. Bake at 350° for 55 minutes or until knife inserted in center comes out clean.

Serves 6.

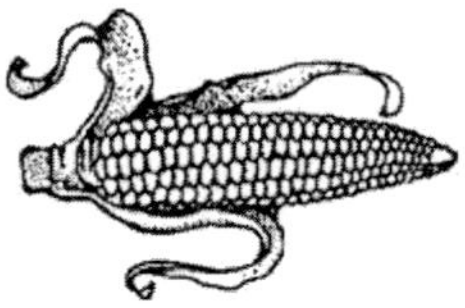

Ham & Corn Fritters

2 EGGS, separated
1/3 cup MILK
1 1/4 cups FLOUR
2 tsp. BAKING POWDER
1 Tbsp. SUGAR
SALT and PEPPER to taste
1 cup CORN KERNELS, cooked and drained
1 cup finely chopped cooked HAM

Combine egg yolks with all ingredients except egg whites and beat until smooth. Beat egg whites until stiff but not dry. Fold egg whites into corn mixture and blend well. With a tablespoon, drop fritter preparation into a skillet of deep, hot oil (375°). Cook until brown. Turn and brown second side.

Serves 4.

Corn Pie

2 Tbsp. BACON DRIPPINGS
3 Tbsp. FLOUR
1 cup MILK
SALT and PEPPER to taste
2 tsp. fresh FINES HERBES BLEND (minced PARSLEY, BASIL, THYME)
3 Tbsp. PARMESAN CHEESE
2 cups CORN KERNELS, cooked and drained
2 med. TOMATOES, sliced 1/4 inch thick
8 slices lean, uncooked BACON, halved
additional PARMESAN CHEESE for garnish

In a medium saucepan, place bacon drippings. Add flour and whip together. Add milk and mix until smooth and thick. Add salt, pepper, herbs and cheese and simmer several minutes. Combine with corn. Pour into a 9-inch buttered pie plate. Arrange sliced tomatoes over entire surface. Sprinkle tomatoes with additional Parmesan cheese. Arrange bacon strips over tomatoes to form a pinwheel. Place one curl of bacon in center of pie. Bake at 350° for 30 minutes. To crisp bacon, place pie under broiler for 2-3 minutes.

Corn & Salmon Casserole

1 can (7 1/4 oz.) SALMON
2 cups CORN KERNELS
1/2 cup diced RED ONION
1 Tbsp. melted BUTTER
1 cup BREAD CRUMBS
2 EGGS, beaten
1 tsp. LEMON JUICE
SALT and PEPPER to taste

Remove skin and small bones from salmon. Mix salmon with corn and onions. Sprinkle melted butter over bread crumbs and toast lightly in oven. Reserve 2 tablespoons crumbs for top of casserole. Mix remaining crumbs with salmon and corn. Add remaining ingredients. Place mixture in a buttered 2-quart casserole and top with reserved crumbs. Bake in a 325° oven for 45 minutes.

Serves 4-6.

Beef & Corn Goulash

4 slices BACON, diced
1/2 cup diced ONION
1 lb. lean GROUND BEEF
2 cups CORN KERNELS
2 cans (16 oz. ea.) diced TOMATOES
SALT and PEPPER to taste

Fry bacon in medium frying pan until almost crisp. Add onion and beef, brown evenly and then pour off drippings. Stir in corn, tomatoes, salt and pepper. Simmer for 45 minutes. Place in greased 2-quart casserole and top with Cornbread Topping. Bake in a 425° oven for 30 minutes.

Serves 8.

Cornbread Topping

1/2 cup YELLOW CORNMEAL
1/2 cup FLOUR
2 Tbsp. SUGAR
2 tsp. BAKING POWDER
1/2 tsp. SALT
1 EGG, beaten
1/2 cup MILK
2 Tbsp. BUTTER, melted
1 can (4 oz.) diced GREEN CHILES, drained

Combine all ingredients and mix until smooth.

Frozen Sweet Corn

12 cups fresh SWEET CORN kernels
3 cups WATER
1/2 cup SUGAR
3 tsp. SALT

Combine all ingredients in a large kettle. Bring mixture to a boil, stirring often. Remove from heat and cool quickly by placing kettle in a sink partly filled with cold water. Change water as needed to assist cooling. Once cool, divide corn and liquids between plastic boxes or plastic bags and freeze.

Corn Chowder

1 (3-inch cube) SALT PORK, diced
1 cup finely chopped ONION
3 cups peeled, diced POTATOES
1/4 cup diced CELERY
3 cups WATER
2 cups CORN KERNELS
3 cups MILK
3 Tbsp. BUTTER
SALT and PEPPER to taste

Cook the salt pork in a 6-quart dutch oven until the fat has melted and slightly browned. Pour off all fat except 2 tablespoonfuls, add the onion and saute until translucent. Add the potatoes, celery and water. Cover and cook until vegetables are tender. Add the corn and milk and cook 10 minutes. Add the butter and seasonings just before serving.

Serves 8-10.

Iowa Corn Pudding

1 can (15 oz.) WHOLE KERNEL CORN, drained
1 can (15 oz.) CREAM-STYLE CORN
4 EGGS, slightly beaten
1/3 cup SUGAR
2 Tbsp. CORNSTARCH
1 tsp. SEASONED SALT
1/2 tsp. DRY MUSTARD
1 tsp. INSTANT ONION POWDER
SALT and PEPPER to taste
1 1/3 cups MILK
1/4 cup melted BUTTER
8 squares SODA CRACKERS, crushed
1/4 cup grated CHEDDAR CHEESE
1/8 cup melted BUTTER

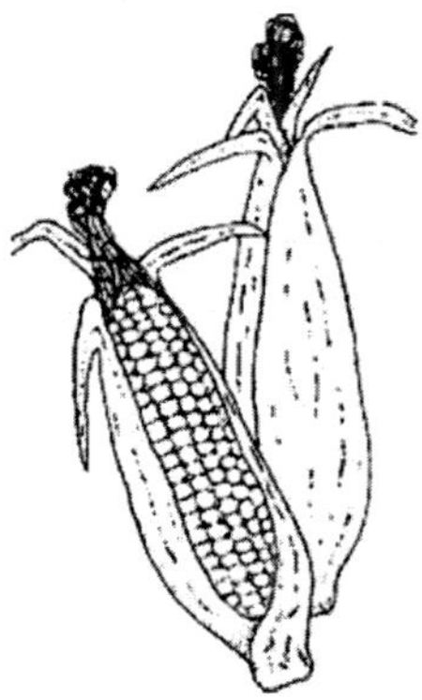

Mix both cans of corn with the eggs. Combine dry ingredients and stir into corn mixture. Add milk and butter. Place in a large, greased casserole dish. Sprinkle crackers, cheese and butter over top. Bake, uncovered, for I hour in a 375° oven. Test for doneness by inserting knife in center; if knife comes out clean, pudding is done.

Serves 8.

Corn Surprise

1 cup CREAM-STYLE CORN
1 cup CORN KERNELS
1/2 cup BUTTER
1 cup cubed AMERICAN CHEESE
1/2 cup diced CELERY
1 cup uncooked broken SPAGHETTI

Mix all ingredients together and pour into a 2-quart casserole. Bake in a 350° oven for 1/2 hour covered and 1/2 hour uncovered.

Creamy Cheese Corn

2 cups CORN KERNELS
1/2 cup WATER
1 pkg. (3 oz.) CREAM CHEESE
1/4 cup CHIVES or FINES HERBES BLEND
(minced PARSLEY, BASIL, THYME)

In a medium saucepan, place corn and water. Add cream cheese and cook on low heat until cheese melts. Add the chives or fines herbes blend.

Country Corn Bread

2 cups YELLOW CORNMEAL
1 cup FLOUR
1 tsp. SALT
1 tsp. SODA
1 tsp. BAKING POWDER
2 EGGS, beaten
2 cups BUTTERMILK
2 Tbsp. COOKING OIL

Combine dry ingredients in a medium bowl. Mix eggs, buttermilk and oil together and add to dry ingredients. Mix well. Pour into a 9 x 9 baking pan or a 12-inch skillet and bake at 375° for 25 to 30 minutes.

Midwest Baked Corn

2 cups CREAM-STYLE CORN
2 cups CORN KERNELS
1 pkg. (8 oz.) CORN MUFFIN MIX
3 EGGS
1/2 cup BUTTER, melted
1 cup SOUR CREAM
1 cup shredded MILD CHEDDAR CHEESE

Mix all ingredients together (except cheese). Pour mixture into a 13 x 9 baking pan and bake at 350° for 15 minutes. Sprinkle cheese over top and continue to bake for an additional 25 minutes or until knife inserted in center comes out clean.

Shoe Peg Casserole

2 Tbsp. BUTTER
2 Tbsp. FLOUR
1 cup WHIPPING CREAM
1 cup CORN KERNELS
SALT and PEPPER to taste

In a medium saucepan, melt butter; blend in flour and stir in cream, corn and seasonings. Put mixture into a baking dish and bake at 350° for 30 minutes.

Corn Filled Green Peppers

6 med. GREEN BELL PEPPERS
3 cups CORN KERNELS
2 EGG YOLKS
1/4 cup MILK
3/4 cup BREAD CRUMBS
SALT and PEPPER to taste
1/2 tsp. SUGAR
2 Tbsp. BUTTER
3 Tbsp. RED PIMENTO

Cut off tops of peppers and remove core and seeds. In a medium bowl, combine corn, egg yolks, milk, bread crumbs, salt, pepper and sugar. Mix well. Spoon mixture into peppers. Top each filled with a slice of butter and garnish with pimentos. Arrange peppers in a 12 x 8 x 2 baking dish. Add a small amount of water to bottom of dish. Bake, uncovered, in a 350° oven for 40 minutes. Baste frequently with juices from bottom of pan.

Serves 6.

Iowa Corn Sticks

1 cup YELLOW CORNMEAL
1/2 cup FLOUR
2 Tbsp. SUGAR
2 tsp. BAKING POWDER
1/2 tsp. SALT
1 EGG, slightly beaten
1/2 cup COOKING OIL
1/2 cup SOUR CREAM
1/2 cup CREAM-STYLE CORN
1 cup CORN KERNELS

In medium bowl, blend together all dry ingredients. Beat egg, oil, sour cream and cream-style corn together. Fold in the corn kernels. Mix all well. Fill greased corn stick pan 3/4 full of batter. Bake in a 400° oven for 12 to 15 minutes.

Makes 12-14 corn sticks.

Hush Puppies

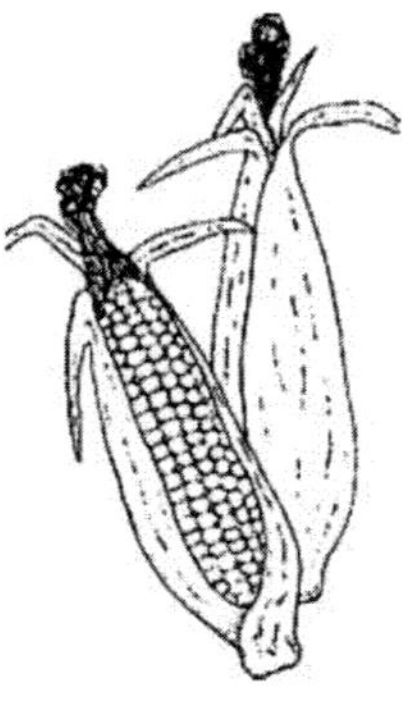

3/4 cup YELLOW CORNMEAL
1/4 cup FLOUR
1 tsp. SUGAR
1 tsp. BAKING POWDER
1/2 tsp. BAKING SODA
3/4 tsp. SALT
1 EGG, slightly beaten
1/2 cup BUTTERMILK
1/4 cup finely chopped ONION
1/8 tsp. chopped CHIVES

In medium bowl, place dry ingredients. Blend egg with buttermilk and add onions and chives. Add the liquid mixture to the dry ingredients. Mix well. Drop by teaspoonful into 375° oil. Fry for 3 minutes, turning to brown all sides evenly. Remove from oil and drain on paper towels.

Serves 4.

Fresh Corn Loaf

2 cups CORN KERNELS
1 cup chopped fresh TOMATOES
1 cup chopped ONION
1 cup chopped GREEN BELL PEPPER
2 tsp. SALT
1/8 tsp. CAYENNE PEPPER
1 cup YELLOW CORNMEAL
1 cup grated CHEDDAR CHEESE
2 EGGS
1/2 cup EVAPORATED MILK
1/2 cup WATER

Mix together corn, tomato, onion, bell pepper, salt, pepper, cornmeal and cheese. Combine and let mixture sit for 30 minutes. Beat eggs, add milk and water and mix well. Add to vegetables, blending together well. Pour into a greased 2-quart. casserole or loaf pan. Bake at 375° for 1 hour.

Serves 6-8.

Lois's Macaroni Bake

1 can (15 oz.) CREAM-STYLE CORN
1 can (15 oz.) WHOLE CORN, undrained
SALT and PEPPER to taste
1 cup uncooked ELBOW MACARONI
2 Tbsp. minced ONION
6 Tbsp. BUTTER
1 cup shredded CHEDDAR CHEESE

Combine all ingredients and place in a greased casserole dish. Bake in a 325° oven for 45 minutes. Stir occasionally while baking. Sprinkle additional grated cheddar cheese on top and return to oven. Continue baking just until cheese has melted and slightly browned.

Serves 4-6.

Breads & Desserts

Danish Rye Bread

"At the Danish Windmill Museum, you can see an authentic 60-foot windmill that was built in Denmark in 1848. The windmill was rebuilt by community volunteers and restored to working condition. The Windmill gift shop is one of the largest Danish import shops in the midwest."

Lisa Riggs-The Danish Windmill, Elk Horn

1 tsp. YEAST
1/4 cup WARM WATER
1 qt. BUTTERMILK
3 Tbsp. MOLASSES
3 Tbsp. LARD
2 tsp. SALT
6 cups RYE GRAHAM FLOUR
6 cups WHOLE-WHEAT FLOUR

Soften yeast in warm water. Heat buttermilk to lukewarm and add to the yeast mixture and stir to mix. Add remaining ingredients and stir well. Knead dough until smooth; let stand overnight. Punch down in the morning. Divide into 3 loaves and let rise in loaf pans for 10 minutes. Bake at 400° for 10 minutes, lower the heat to 250° and continue baking for 1 3/4 hours. Place a cookie sheet over the pans and weigh down while baking. When cool, slice into very thin slices.

Oatmeal-Apple Bread

"Fun to make, tasty, and oh so healthy!
Leftovers (if any) make great French toast."
Barbara Stensvad-Chestnut Charm Bed & Breakfast, Atlantic

1/3 cup RAISINS
2 Tbsp. RUM
1 tsp. SUGAR
1/3 cup (packed) BROWN SUGAR
2 Tbsp. MOLASSES
1 Tbsp. SALT
1 3/4 cups unsweetened APPLE JUICE or APPLE CIDER
2 Tbsp. melted BUTTER
5 1/2 to 6 cups BREAD FLOUR
2 pkg. active DRY YEAST
1/2 tsp. ground CINNAMON
1 1/2 cups regular ROLLED OATS
3/4 cup finely chopped APPLE
1/2 cup chopped WALNUTS
1 EGG WHITE blended with 1 Tbsp. WATER for glaze

In a small bowl, mix raisins and rum. Cover and set aside 3-4 hours or overnight to soak. In a saucepan, mix both sugars, molasses, salt, juice and butter. Heat until warm. In a medium bowl, place 3 cups of bread flour, yeast and cinnamon and mix with hand mixer. Add sugar mixture and mix well. Add oats, apple and walnuts and mix. Slowly add remaining flour (just to make a soft dough). Turn out dough onto a lightly floured surface. Knead 8-10 minutes or until dough is smooth and elastic. Place dough in a large greased bowl, turning to grease all sides. Let rise until double in a warm, moist oven or draft-free corner. After dough has risen, punch down and knead for 30 seconds. Divide dough and place in 3 greased loaf pans. Let rise again until double. Preheat oven to 375°. Gently move pans to oven. Bake 35-40 minutes or until bread sounds hollow when tapped on bottom. After the first 15 minutes of baking, brush with egg-white glaze. If bread is browning too quickly, put a foil tent over top. Remove from pans and cool on racks.

Danish Kringle

"This is a good Danish recipe that I have used for many years."
Peggy Hansen-Hansen's Kro Bed & Breakfast, Elk Horn

4 cups FLOUR
3 Tbsp. SUGAR
1 tsp. SALT
1 cup BUTTER-FLAVOR CRISCO®
1 cup MILK
1 pkg. granular YEAST
1 tsp. SUGAR
1/2 cup lukewarm WATER
3 EGG YOLKS, beaten
FILLING of choice

In a large bowl, cream flour, sugar, salt and Crisco. Scald milk and cool to lukewarm. Dissolve yeast and 1 teaspoonful sugar in the 1/2 cup lukewarm water. Combine milk, yeast, and egg yolks. Work into the flour mixture, making a soft dough. Cover and refrigerate overnight. Next day, divide the dough into four parts and roll each into strips about 9 inches wide. Spread with your favorite filling (apricot, prune, etc.). Fold a third of the dough over the filling. Place on a well greased baking sheet. Set in a warm place, cover, and let rise until very puffy. Bake in a 350° oven until light golden brown. Frost with your favorite frosting.

Irish Soda Bread

"Both my husband and I are from Northern Ireland. This bread was baked regularly in my home there. Nowadays, we often serve this bread to our guests."
Dorothy Spriggs-Carriage House Bed and Breakfast, Grinnell

1 1/2 cups FLOUR
1 tsp. BAKING SODA
1/2 tsp. SALT
1 cup BUTTERMILK

Mix dry ingredients together. Add the buttermilk all at once and mix to a soft dough with a knife. Turn out onto a floured surface and knead very lightly. Pat into a circle about 1/2" thick. Cut into 4 pie-shaped quarters (farls). In a skillet*, over medium-high heat, bake bread on both sides until crispy and brown. Cut each farl in half, so that you now have 8 farls. Slice each farl horizontally, butter the cut sides and serve.

* If using an electric skillet, set heat at 375° to bake farls.

Round 'n' Brown Coffee Can Bread

"This recipe was developed to teach 4th graders about making bread and the importance of whole wheat. Thousands of southwest Iowa students successfully made this bread. Many adult groups also use this recipe."

LaVon Eblen-Host of Backyard & Beyond radio show, KJAD, Atlantic

2 cups WHOLE WHEAT FLOUR
2 cups WHITE FLOUR
1 pkg. DRY YEAST
1 cup NONFAT DRY MILK
3 Tbsp. SUGAR
1/2 tsp. SALT
1 3/4 cups + 2 Tbsp. warm WATER
1/4 cup OIL

Place all dry ingredients in a gallon, pressure-sealed bag and seal. Rotate bag to blend dry ingredients. Open bag and add warm water and oil. Press out as much air as possible and then seal bag. Squeeze bag until all ingredients are moistened, bubbles begin to form and dough is no longer sticking to sides of bag. Divide dough evenly between two, well-greased 1-pound coffee cans. Snap on well-greased plastic lids. When lids pop off, (about 1 hour), place cans in a 375° oven and bake for 35 minutes. Remove cans immediately and cool on racks.

Note: This recipe may also be mixed in a bowl and baked in two 8x4 loaf pans.

The Mound Builders

Iowa was once the home of prehistoric Indians called Mound Builders; they had disappeared long before the first settlers arrived in 1673 but left behind over 10,000 burial mounds containing tools and weapons.

Helga's Peach Pie

"We maintain a family farm in southwest Iowa. We raise hogs, cows, corn, soybeans, hay and oats."

Dan, Barb & Tony Smith-Exira

4 cups sliced fresh PEACHES
1 cup SUGAR
1 1/2 Tbsp. LEMON JUICE
3 Tbsp. TAPIOCA
1/8 tsp. CINNAMON
1/4 tsp. SALT
1 1/2 Tbsp. BUTTER
2 (9-inch) unbaked PIE CRUSTS

In a medium bowl, combine peaches, sugar, lemon juice, tapioca, cinnamon and salt. Blend well together. Turn into a 9-inch pie crust. Dot with butter. Place remaining crust on top and vent with the tines of a fork. Bake in a 350° oven for 1 hour.

Strawberry-Rhubarb Pie

"Our town is the home of the "World's Largest Strawberry' (fifteen feet high and twelve feet wide), gateway to Backbone State Park and known as the 'Little Switzerland of America.'"

Charlotte Fliehler-Secretary of the Strawberry Point Chamber of Commerce, Strawberry Point

1 1/2 cups SUGAR
3 Tbsp. TAPIOCA
1/4 tsp. SALT
1/4 tsp. NUTMEG
1 cup sliced STRAWBERRIES
3 cups RHUBARB, cut into 1/2 inch pieces
1 Tbsp. BUTTER
2 (9-inch) unbaked PIE CRUSTS

In a medium bowl, combine sugar, tapioca, salt and nutmeg, and blend together. Add strawberries and rhubarb and stir just enough to coat fruit. Allow to stand about 20 minutes. Pour mixture into unbaked crust. Dot with butter. Slice remaining crust and place slices, lattice-style, over pie mixture. Bake in a 400° oven for 35 to 40 minutes.

Sweet Cream
(Dolci Panna)

"This is a simple recipe to make, and a great dessert!"
Terry Lowman-Lucullan's Italian Grill, Ames

1/2 cup SUGAR
1 tsp. WATER
2 cups CREAM
2 cups MILK
1 1/8 cups SUGAR
3 1/2 tsp. GELATIN

In a saucepan, heat 1/2 cup sugar and water until brown. Divide sugar mixture between 8 warmed custard dishes and set aside to cool. Heat cream and milk to boiling in a saucepan. Combine 11/8 cups sugar and gelatin together and stir into cream. Set saucepan in a larger pan that has been layered with ice and cool thoroughly. Pour cooled milk mixture into a small pitcher or measuring cup and pour over caramelized sugar in custard dishes. Chill. To serve; dip bottom of custard dishes in hot water and turn over onto serving plate.

Best Ever Raisin Pie

"My mother-in-law made this pie often, and she swore that the dab of butter added at the end was what made this the 'Best Ever Raisin Pie.'"
Connie Maneman-Storm Lake

1 cup RAISINS
1 1/2-2 cups WATER
2 EGG YOLKS, beaten
1/4 cup SUGAR
1/4 cup FLOUR
1/2 cup MILK
1 tsp. VANILLA
1/4 tsp. CINNAMON
1 Tbsp. BUTTER
1 baked PIE CRUST
WHIPPED CREAM

In small saucepan combine raisins with water (just enough water to cover). Simmer gently until raisins are plump. Drain. In a medium bowl, combine egg yolks, sugar, flour, milk, vanilla and cinnamon and beat well. Add to raisins in saucepan. Cook mixture over low heat until bubbly and thick (about 1 minute). Add that special dab ofbutter and blend in. Cool mixture slightly and pour into baked pie crust shell. Top with whipped cream or a meringue.

Peanut Butter Chocolate Chip Cheesecake

"Allamakee County is in the far northeast corner of our state and is one of Iowa's most scenic counties."

Kari Kelly-Waukon

1 1/4 cups GRAHAM CRACKER crumbs
1/3 cup SUGAR
1/4 cup COCOA
1/4 cup BUTTER or MARGARINE
3 pkgs. (8 oz. ea.) CREAM CHEESE, softened
1 can SWEETENED CONDENSED MILK
1 2/3 cups PEANUT BUTTER CHIPS, melted
4 EGGS, beaten
2 tsp. VANILLA EXTRACT
1 cup mini-sized, SEMI-SWEET CHOCOLATE CHIPS

In medium bowl combine graham cracker crumbs, sugar, cocoa and butter or margarine. Press graham cracker mixture into the bottom of a 9-inch springform pan. In a large mixing bowl, beat together cream cheese and condensed milk. Add peanut butter chips, eggs and vanilla extract. Beat well. Fold in the chocolate chips and pour mixture into the crumb crust. Bake in a 325° oven for 55-60 minutes or until center is set. Cool and refrigerate. Garnish as desired.

Hint: Usually the cheesecake top splits when it is done. Tip pan side to side very gently, and if the center of the cake is not firm, keep baking.

Tin Roof Mousse Pie

"Waterloo Museum of Art is a permanent, nonprofit institution dedicated to furthering community awareness and appreciation for the arts, through acquiring, preserving, exhibiting and interpreting works of art."

Terry Poe Buschkam
Waterloo Convention & Visitors Bureau, Waterloo

Crust:

1 1/2 cups cream-filled CHOCOLATE COOKIES, crumbled
4-6 Tbsp. BUTTER, melted

Filling:

1/2 cup BUTTER, softened
3/4 cup SUGAR
2 squares UNSWEETENED CHOCOLATE, melted, cooled
2 EGGS
2 cups WHIPPED TOPPING
1/3 cup PEANUT BUTTER CHIPS
1/3 cup CHOCOLATE CHIPS

Topping:

1 Tbsp. POWDERED SUGAR
1 cup WHIPPING CREAM
SPANISH PEANUTS
COOKIE CRUMBS

In a medium bowl, combine crumbled chocolate cookies with melted butter. Press into a buttered 9-inch pie pan. In mixer bowl, cream softened butter with sugar and add the melted chocolate. Add eggs, one at a time, and beat for 5 minutes. Fold in whipped topping, peanut butter chips and chocolate chips. Pour into cookie crust. Chill for two hours. Whip together the powdered sugar and whipping cream until firm. Pour over dessert and garnish with peanuts and cookie crumbs.

Waterloo

Places to visit in Waterloo:

- *Bluedorn Science Imaginarium*
- *Grout Museum of History and Science*
- *Rensselaer Russell House Museum,*
- *Waterloo Museum of Art*

Chocolate Pizza

Theresa Phillips-Tanger Outlet Center, Williamsburg

1 pkg. SEMI-SWEET CHOCOLATE CHIPS
1 lb. WHITE ALMOND BARK, divided
2 cups MINIATURE MARSHMALLOWS
1 cup RICE KRISPIES cereal
1 cup PEANUTS
1 jar (6 oz.) RED MARASCHINO CHERRIES, drained and halved
3 Tbsp. GREEN MARASCHINO CHERRIES, drained and quartered
1/ 3 cup COCONUT
1 tsp. OIL

In a 2-quart microwave-safe bowl, combine chocolate chips and 14 ounces (7 squares) of the almond bark. Microwave on high for 2 minutes. Stir and continue microwaving for 1 to 2 minutes until mixture is smooth (stirring every 30 seconds). Stir in marshmallows, cereal and peanuts. Pour onto greased 12-inch pizza pan. Top with red and green cherries and sprinkle with coconut. In a small bowl, microwave remaining 2 ounces almond bark (1 square) and oil, for 1 minute. Stir. Continue microwaving 30 seconds to 1 minute or until smooth when stirred (stirring every 15 seconds). Drizzle over coconut and refrigerate pizza until firm. Store at room temperature. To serve, cut into pizza-style wedges.

Serves 12.

Iowa City

Home to the University of Iowa and its unusual Iowa Hospitals and Clinics Medical Museum. The museum includes two galleries that feature exhibitions on the history of medicine. A large art collection is on display throughout the hospital. On 1-80, just west of Iowa City and sister city Coralville, can be found the Coral Ridge Mall which is considered to be the largest mall in Iowa.

Encore Chocolate-Coconut Cake

(Dad's favorite)

"The city of Coralville, a hub of hospitality, offers many lodgings and fine restaurants, besides being a place of great recreational opportunity. We celebrated our 125th anniversary in 1998."

Mayor Jim I. Fausett–Coralville

1 pkg. WHITE CAKE MIX
2 squares grated BAKER'S® UNSWEETENED CHOCOLATE
1 1/3 cups BAKER'S® ANGEL FLAKE COCONUT
1 lg. ctn. COOL WHIP®

Prepare cake mix as directed on package. Fold in grated chocolate. (I add grated chocolate to only one pan.) Bake in two round 9-inch pans. Split cooled layers horizontally. Add coconut to Cool Whip and spread between three layers and on top. Spread Encore Chocolate Frosting on sides. Garnish top with coconut.

Encore Chocolate Frosting

2 squares BAKER'S® UNSWEETENED CHOCOLATE
1 cup plus 2 Tbsp. sifted POWDERED SUGAR
2 Tbsp. HOT WATER
1 EGG YOLK
3 Tbsp. BUTTER

Melt chocolate, remove from heat and place in a small bowl. Add sugar and water and blend well. Beat in egg and add butter one tablespoon at a time. Blend until smooth.

Cream Puff Dessert

"I first made this dessert for a church dinner. It is now a favorite of my family and is often requested."

Lorraine Christiansen-Christiansen Family Farm, Denison

1 cup WATER
1/2 cup MARGARINE
1 cup FLOUR
4 EGGS
2 pkgs (3.5 oz. ea.) INSTANT VANILLA PUDDING
3 cups MILK
1 pkg. (8 oz.) CREAM CHEESE, softened
COOL WHIP®
1/8 cup CHOCOLATE SYRUP

In a medium size saucepan, blend water and margarine and bring to a boil. Add flour and beat until mixture forms a firm ball. Remove from heat and add eggs, one at a time, beating well after each. Spread mixture in a 13 x 9 pan and bake in a 375° oven for 40 minutes. Cool. In a medium size bowl, blend pudding with milk. Mix well. Add softened cream cheese and blend together well. Allow to set for 10 minutes before spreading over crust. Spread Cool Whip over pudding and drizzle chocolate syrup over top.

Ammonia Cookies

"My Grandmother brought this recipe from Germany in 1899. These cookies are unique and delicious."

Gen Baker-Denison

1 cup BUTTER very soft
2 tsp. BAKING AMMONIA
1 tsp. CARDAMOM
1 cup SUGAR
2 cups FLOUR

In a mixer bowl, cream all ingredients together. Form into small balls with your hands and place on a cookie sheet. Bake in a 325° oven only until light tan in color (6-7 minutes). Do not brown, they will crack!

Note: Baking ammonia is purchased at drug stores and some bakeries.

Strawberry Pizza

"Campers' Gateway to the Amana Colonies."
Darlene M. Nielsen
Sleepy Hollow RV Park & Campground, Oxford

1 tube of PILLSBURY® COOKIE DOUGH
1 pkg. (8 oz.) CREAM CHEESE
3/4 tsp. VANILLA
1/3 cup BROWN SUGAR
1 container (8 oz.) COOL WHIP®
fresh STRAWBERRIES

Lightly grease a jellyroll pan and pat cookie dough into bottom of pan to form a crust. Bake crust ten minutes in a 425° oven. Let cool. In a medium bowl, combine cream cheese, vanilla, sugar, and Cool Whip. Spread on top of cooled crust. Distribute fresh strawberries over surface. Top with Strawberry Pizza Sauce and refrigerate overnight or for several hours. Serve with dollops of Cool Whip on top.

Strawberry Pizza Sauce

1 1/2 cups WATER
2 Tbsp. CORNSTARCH
3/4 cup SUGAR
1 pkg. (3 oz.) WILD STRAWBERRY JELL-O®

In a medium saucepan, combine water, cornstarch and sugar. Cook and stir mixture until clear. Add Jell-0 and mix well. Cook until Jell-0 is completely dissolved. Cool.

Amana Colonies
Seven Old-World Villages

The early settlers of the Amana Colonies left Germany in 1842, settling near Buffalo, New York. In need of more land the community moved west in 1855. The Amana Colonies were based on tradition and quality. This indelible mark of craftsmanship can still be seen in the products made today in the Amana Colonie's furniture and clock factories, woolen mills, and shops.

Rhubarb Dessert

"My mother was a cook at the Audubon Hospital, and then again at the Friendship Home here in Audubon. This dessert was a favorite and requested often. It is also my family's favorite and is always a hit at our potluck dinners."

Norma Hansen-Audubon

4 cups chopped RHUBARB
1 1/2 cups SUGAR
2 Tbsp. MINUTE TAPIOCA
1 cup BROWN SUGAR
1/2 cup MARGARINE
1 EGG
1 cup FLOUR
1/2 tsp. BAKING POWDER
1/2 cup MILK

In medium bowl, combine rhubarb, sugar and tapioca. Spread over the bottom of a greased 13 x 9 baking pan. In a mixing bowl, cream brown sugar with margarine. Add egg and stir until well blended. Add flour, baking powder and milk. Mix well and pour over the rhubarb mixture. Bake in a 350° oven for 45 minutes.

Banana Cake

Davenport Museum of Art features collections of American, European and Regionalist art, including Grant Wood, Mexican Colonial Paintings and Haitian art of the naive tradition-plus the biannual (May & Sept.) outdoor Beaux Arts Fair.

Steve Bradley-Director, Davenport Museum of Art, Davenport

1/2 cup MARGARINE
1 1/2 cups SUGAR
1/2 cup SOUR MILK
2 EGGS
1 cup MASHED BANANAS
1/2 tsp. BAKING SODA
1 tsp. VANILLA
1/4 tsp. LEMON EXTRACT
1/2 cup NUTMEATS
2 cups FLOUR
1 tsp. BAKING POWDER
1/4 tsp. SALT

In mixer bowl, combine margarine and sugar. Cream well together. Add remaining ingredients and beat two minutes. Pour into a greased 13x9 cake pan. Bake in a 325° oven for 25-30 minutes. Serve plain or top with whipped cream or, our favorite, a powdered sugar frosting.

Ostakaka

"All of my husband's great-grandparents emigrated from Sweden. This recipe came from a friend of my husband's grandmother. I first made it 54 years ago."

Audrienne Swedlund-Stratford

1 cup FLOUR
1 cup MILK
dash of SALT
1 tsp. LIQUID RENNET or
1 RENNET TABLET dissolved in a small amount of water
3 EGGS
1 cup SUGAR
2 cups CREAM
1 gal. MILK

Combine flour, 1 cup milk and salt together to form a paste. Heat the gallon of milk to lukewarm. Add the flour paste and liquid rennet (or dissolved rennet tablet) to the milk. Heat and stir until milk thickens and curds appear. Remove from heat and let stand until whey appears. Drain off most of the whey. Beat eggs; add the cream and sugar and blend. Pour egg mixture over curds. Stir gently. Pour into 13 x 9 baking pan, or large casserole dish. Bake at 375° for one hour, or until firm (like a custard) and an inserted knife comes out clean.

Amish Peanut Butter Spread

"Kalona is home to the largest Amish community west of the Mississippi River."

Sally Kern-Kalona Area Chamber of Commerce, Kalona

1 cup WATER
2 cups BROWN SUGAR
2 Tbsp. WHITE SYRUP
1 tsp. MAPLE FLAVORING
1 pt. MARSHMALLOW CREME
2 cups PEANUT BUTTER

Bring water, brown sugar, syrup and maple flavoring to a boil. Remove from heat and cool. Mix in marshmallow creme and peanut butter.

Apple Danish Bars

Mary Mallet, Food Chemist-Sioux Honey Association, Sioux City

3 cups FLOUR
1/2 tsp. SALT
1 cup VEGETABLE SHORTENING
1 EGG, separated
1/2 cup MILK
6 cups peeled and sliced APPLES
3/4 cup SUE BEE® HONEY
1/4 cup FLOUR
1/4 cup MARGARINE
1/2 tsp. SALT
3/4 cup SUGAR
1 tsp. CINNAMON

Cream flour, salt and shortening until crumbly. Combine beaten egg yolk and milk, blend into flour mixture. Divide dough in half and roll out each half to fit a 15 x 10 jellyroll pan. Place one half of dough in pan. Arrange apples over top and drizzle with honey. Combine remaining ingredients (except egg white) and sprinkle over apples. Place second crust on top and brush with beaten egg white. Bake in a 375° oven for 45 minutes. Drizzle with the Powdered Sugar Glaze while still warm.

Powdered Sugar Glaze

1 1/2 cups POWDERED SUGAR
1 tsp. VANILLA
Dash of SALT
2-3 Tbsp. MILK

Blend sugar, vanilla and salt together. Add enough milk to form a smooth, spreadable glaze.

Sioux Honey Association

With $200 and 3000 pounds of honey, five beekeepers located near Sioux City formed a cooperative marketing organization in 1921. Sioux Honey Association has become a worldwide marketing organization, and it continues to be a leader in the honey industry with state of the art facilities and labor and developmental research.

Maple Walnut Chippers

"The sap collected from the Hartman sugarbush is boiled down in our sugar shack to make the syrup (the sap is mostly water). Approximately 40 gallons of sap boils down to only one gallon of syrup! The syrup we make here at Hartman reserve is used at our annual Maple Syrup Festival, held the first Saturday in March."

Linette Riley, Special Events Coordinator
Hartman Reserve Nature Center, Cedar Falls

2 1/4 cups FLOUR
1 tsp. BAKING SODA
1/2 tsp. SALT
1 cup BUTTER or MARGARINE
1/2 cup GRANULATED SUGAR
1/2 cup firmly packed BROWN SUGAR
1/4 cup MAPLE SYRUP
1 EGG
1/2 cup coarsely chopped WALNUTS
2 cups or 1 pkg. (12 oz.) SEMI-SWEET CHOCOLATE CHIPS

In medium size bowl, combine flour, soda and salt. Set aside. In mixer bowl, cream butter (or margarine) and sugars. Add maple syrup and egg, blend well. Blend in flour mixture. Mix well. Stir in nuts and chocolate chips. Drop by teaspoonfuls onto ungreased baking sheets. Bake in a 375° oven for 8-10 minutes, until golden brown. Cool for a few minutes on cookie sheet then remove to rack.

Cedar Falls

Interesting places to visit in Cedar Falls:

- *George Wyth House and Viking Pump Museum*
- *Hartman Reserve Nature Center*
- *Ice House Museum*
- *James & Meryl Hearst Center for the Arts*
- *Little Red Schoolhouse*
- *University of Northern Iowa Gallery of Art*
- *Victorian Home & Carriage House Museum*

Rhubarb Shortcake

"The old-fashioned name for rhubarb was 'pie plant'. When I was young, we lived on a farm with plenty of rhubarb in the garden and all the milk we wanted thanks to our milking cows. We always had fresh cream for this shortcake!"

Audrienne Swedlund-Stratford

1 cup SUGAR
1 cup SOUR CREAM
1 1/2 cups FLOUR
1 tsp. BAKING SODA
1/2 tsp. BAKING POWDER
1 1/4 tsp. SALT
2 cups RHUBARB

In a large bowl, combine all ingredients (except rhubarb). Combine well. Fold in rhubarb. Pour mixture into a floured cake pan and bake in a 350° oven for about 30 minutes.

Aunt Lucy's Caramel Corn

"Our Uncle, Jack May (ofExira), was called 'The Popcorn King.' He contracted with farmers in southwestern Iowa to grow popcorn and he was a broker of popcorn to several large popcorn companies. He also raised popcorn. His wife, Lucy, has always made this wonderful caramel corn and shared her recipe with family members. For years, Jack donated sacks of popcorn to many area schools and events."

Alice May-Audubon

2 cups BROWN SUGAR
1/2 cup CORN SYRUP
1 cup MARGARINE
3/4 tsp. SALT
1 tsp. BAKING SODA
1 tsp. BURNT SUGAR FLAVORING
1 tsp. BUTTER FLAVORING
jumbo WHITE SALTED PEANUTS, shelled
8 qts. POPCORN

In heavy saucepan, combine sugar, syrup, margarine and salt. Bring to a boil and cook 5 minutes. Remove from heat and add baking soda, flavorings and peanuts. Pour mixture over popcorn. Turn into greased cake pans. Bake in 250° oven for 1 hour, stirring every 15 minutes. (Oven racks should be placed in middle of oven.)

Microwaved Popcorn Balls

Terri W. Rininger-Midnight Sun, Schaller

1 1/2 cups SUGAR
1 cup WHITE SYRUP
1/2 cup BUTTER
2 Tbsp. VINEGAR
7 qts. popped POPCORN
chopped NUTS

In a medium bowl, combine sugar, syrup, butter and vinegar. Microwave 5 minutes. Stir. Microwave an additional 4 minutes. Add nuts and color if desired. Pour over popped corn, stir until all are well-coated.

Christmas Popcorn Balls

"Schaller, Iowa, celebrates 'Popcorn Days' every summer. Good entertainment and free popcorn is enjoyed at this festival.

Theresa Bailey-Schaller Herald, Schaller

3 1/2 qts. popped POPCORN
1 pkg. RED or GREEN GELATIN
1 cup WHITE CORN SYRUP
1/2 cup SUGAR

Place popcorn in a large container. In a medium saucepan, combine gelatin, syrup and sugar. Heat to boiling stage, but do not boil. Remove from heat and cool for one minute before pouring over popcorn. Stir until well coated. When popcorn is cool, butter your hands and shape popcorn into balls. If popcorn doesn't stick together it may be too hot, let it cool a few minutes.

Pink Popcorn Balls

"I have made this recipe for over 50 years. My grandchildren especially like the food coloring addition."

Ruth Borcherding-Schaller

1 1/2 cups WHITE SUGAR
1 cup WHITE SYRUP
1/2 cup BUTTER OR MARGARINE
2 Tbsp. VINEGAR
RED FOOD COLORING
6 qts. popped POPCORN

Combine all ingredients in a medium size saucepan. Boil until soft ball forms. Use enough red food coloring to make the mixture pink. Fill a 6-quart bowl with popped popcorn and pour sugar mixture over all, stirring to cover.

Index

Index (continued from previous page)

Index (continued from previous page)

Index (continued from previous page)

About the Author

Dorothy Smith is a lifetime resident of west-central Iowa. She and her husband, Duane, raised their five children on the family farm in Audubon county.

Herself a member of a large farm family, Dorothy learned "feed-the-hungry" skills at an early age. As the wife of a farmer, regular announcements like "corn sheller crew for lunch" gave her ample practice in all aspects of the culinary trade.

Dorothy and Duane opened the John James Audubon Bed & Breakfast in Audubon, Iowa, in 1991 and published the John James Audubon Bed & Breakfast Cookbook in 1998, featuring the foods they prepared and served to their guests.

Recipe:

From:

Ingredients:

Directions:

Recipe:

From:

Ingredients:

Directions:

Salsa Lovers Cookbook

More than 180 recipes for salsa, dips, salads, appetizers and more!

$9.95

Quick-n-Easy Mexican Recipes

Make your favorite Mexican dishes in record time! Excellent tacos, tostadas, enchiladas and more!

$9.95

Chip and Dip Lovers Cookbook

Easy and colorful recipes from Southwestern salsas to quick appetizer dips!

$9.95

Tortilla Lovers' Cookbook

Celebrate the tortilla with more than 100 easy recipes for breakfast, lunch, dinner, appetizers and desserts, too!

$9.95

Chili Lovers Cookbook

Prize-winning recipes for chili, with or without beans. Plus a variety of taste-tempting foods made with flavorful chile peppers.

$9.95

Arizona Cookbook

A collection of more than 350 authentic Arizona recipes. Including Indian, Mexican. and Western foods.

$9.95

New Mexico Cookbook

This unique book explores the age-old recipes that are rich with the heritage of New Mexico.

$9.95

Easy RV Recipes

Easy recipes for the traveling cook. Over 200 recipes to make in your RV, camper or houseboat.

$9.95

Easy Recipes for Wild Game

More than 200 "wild" recipes for large and small game, wild fowl and fish.

$9.95

Apple Lovers Cookbook

What's more American than eating apple pie? Try these 150 favorite recipes for appetizers, main and side dishes, muffins, pies, salads, beverages and preserves.

$9.95

Pumpkin Lovers Cookbook

More than 175 recipes for soups, breads, muffins, pies, cakes, cheesecakes, cookies and even ice cream! Carving tips, trivia and more.

$9.95

Mexican Family Favorites Recipes

250 authentic, homestyle recipes for tacos, tamales, menudo, enchiladas, burros, salsas, frijoles, carne seca, chile rellenos, guacamole, and more!

$9.95

ORDER BLANK

GOLDEN WEST PUBLISHERS

5738 North Central Avenue • Phoenix, AZ 85012

www.goldenwestpublishers.com • 1-800-521-9221 • FAX 602-234-3062

Qty	Title	Price	Amount
	Apple Lovers Cookbook	9.95	
	Arizona Cookbook	9.95	
	Bean Lovers Cookbook	9.95	
	Best Barbecue Recipes	14.95	
	Chili-Lovers' Cookbook	9.95	
	Chip and Dip Lovers Cookbook	9.95	
	Cowboy Cookbook	9.95	
	Easy Recipes for Wild Game	9.95	
	Easy RV Recipes	9.95	
	Grand Canyon Cookbook	9.95	
	Low Fat Mexican Recipes	9.95	
	New Mexico Cookbook	9.95	
	Mexican Family Favorites Cookbook	9.95	
	Peach Lovers Cookbook	9.95	
	Pecan Lovers Cookbook	9.95	
	Quick-n-Easy Mexican Recipes	9.95	
	Salsa Lovers Cookbook	9.95	
	Seafood Lovers Cookbook	9.95	
	Sedona Cookbook	9.95	
	Tequila Cookbook	9.95	
	Texas Cookbook	9.95	
	Tortilla Lovers Cookbook	9.95	
	Veggie Lovers Cookbook	9.95	

U.S. Shipping & Handling Add: (Shipping to all other countries see website.)	1-3 Books $5.00 4+ Books $7.00	
	Arizona residents add 8.1% sales tax	

Total $________

(Payable in U.S. funds)

☐ My Check or Money Order Enclosed

☐ MasterCard ☐ VISA ☐ Discover ☐ American Express Verification code______

Acct. No. ________________________ Exp. Date __________

Signature ________________________

Name ________________________ Phone __________

Address ________________________

City/State/Zip ________________________

Call for a FREE catalog of all our titles — Prices subject to change —